Allen & Mike's Real
BACKPACK
BOOK

Traveling & camping skills for a wilderness environment!

RIGHT ON!

Allen O'Bannon
& illustrations by Mike Clelland!

FALCONGUIDE®

GUILFORD, CONNECTICUT
HELENA, MONTANA

AN IMPRINT OF THE GLOBE PEQUOT PRESS

A FALCON GUIDE®

Cover illustration by Mike Clelland!

Library of Congress Cataloging-in-Publication Data
O'Bannon, Allen.
    Allen and Mike's really cool backpackin' book / by Allen
O'Bannon and Mike Clelland.
        p. cm.
    ISBN-13: 978-1-56044-912-6

    1. Backpacking. I. Clelland, Mike. II. Title.
  GV199.6.O23 2001
  796.51—dc21

                                        00-051867

♻ Text pages printed on recycled paper.
Manufactured in the United States of America
First Edition/Eighth Publishing

> To buy books in quantity for corporate use
> or incentives, call **(800) 962–0973**
> or e-mail **premiums@GlobePequot.com.**

Contents

Acknowledgments

Oh my gosh. There are so many people whom I have learned from, that it would be a separate book unto itself to name them all. As a student of and instructor for the National Outdoor Leadership School, I gained an incredible depth of knowledge from all the wonderful people who work there. This is the place where I truly honed my skills and gained much of my experience and wisdom. Thanks to all those I have worked with and to all of their mentors as well. All of our experience is built on those who came before.

Many thanks to all my friends from high school and college who got me started in the outdoors. It was in these early years that I gained appreciation for and inspiration from the natural world and all its beauty.

Thanks to Mike Clelland for his wonderful and inspiring illustrations, for all the editing that he did, and for getting me started as a writer. Also thanks to John Burbidge, our editor at Falcon, for helping us along. Finally thanks to Erika Eschholz for the time and understanding she gave me in order to complete this project.

Allen O'Bannon

A Note from Mike!

Why go into the wilderness? The natural world can be hard work, frustrating, and uncomfortable . . . but we go nonetheless. What pulls us there, to a place that we sometimes perceive as unwelcoming? For me, and maybe you too, there is a very real tugging at the soul, a deep-rooted desire to find something, to achieve something . . . a metaphysical fix of some sort.

The oppressive influences of our modern society keep many of us from being our real selves. We continually react not to Mother Nature, but to Mother Culture, and we take on identities and personalities not our own. But when we step into the wilderness, we temporarily liberate ourselves from those influences. There is a very real value to time spent in the wilderness. Perhaps we can begin to discover a little more about our real selves. Maybe we'll get some reassurance that there is something behind it all, and that it's good.

I spend up to 30 days at a time in the wilderness, instructing for an outdoor school, and many of my fellow travelers are new to the Grand Experience of wilderness travel. They'll often excitedly vocalize their observations with statements like: "We are in the middle of nowhere!"; "There is nothing out here!"; and, "Y'know, back in the real world . . ."

I have learned that it's impossible to be nowhere, much less in the middle of it. Wherever you are, and most especially in the wilderness, you are quite definitely—somewhere!

In the backcountry, you are surrounded not by nothing, but by lots and lots of something, an amazing variety of the inter-locking everything!

Don't look away over the distant horizon for someplace called the "real world." That is the illusion. Wherever you are, any place your feet are planted on this fabulously complex and beautiful earth, you are—most assuredly—in the Real World.

     Mike Clelland!

Introduction: Camping in Style

A simple equation exists between freedom and numbers: the more people the less freedom.

Royal Robbins, Basic Rockcraft

Style is everything, especially in the backcountry. This has nothing to do with how you dress or what type of gear you have. We're not talking about fashion—rather, how you act, carry yourself, and camp. For example, being a bombproof camper and knowing where all your gear is at any one time. Not having stuff hanging all over the outside of your pack, waiting to get pulled off or broken. Being considerate to the other campers you run into. This is all good style. Staying warm and dry while everyone else is stumbling around wet and cold is good style. So is keeping a positive attitude on the rare occasions when you hiked 5 miles in the wrong direction. It is stuff like this that defines a good outdoorsperson. Striving to camp and travel in good style makes you a better camper in the long run.

Good style helps define a set of ethics for us as outdoor users. No longer can we simply do whatever we please in the woods. With so many other users, we need a set of principles or standards to help govern our actions. With so many humans traveling the confined spaces of our planet's undeveloped places, we need a way to protect the land and other resources so they remain substantially unchanged. If we as campers practice and develop the skills to keep pristine areas free of impact, then the government doesn't need to regulate us. We must take personal responsibility for our actions and do more than just follow a bunch of regulations meant to protect us, others, and the land. This is what ethics are all about.

Our goal as backcountry travelers must be to minimize our impact through the way we interact with the land and its inhabitants. Can we leave it unimpaired for future visitors, be they us in another five years, or our children and their grandchildren? Wilderness will never be the way it was when Lewis and Clark first traveled across North America. And 100 years in the future it will probably be substantially different than it is now. However, if we practice minimum-impact skills and act to protect wild places in all facets of our lives, wilderness will still exist.

Some of the practices I talk about are more about courtesy to others than anything else. Some are just techniques designed to make you a better camper. Other practices help to minimize the effect you have on the land, whether you recognize it or not. Take the time to consider and accept those techniques and practices that ring true to you. If you are unsure of something, don't blow it off as the opinion of some crazy zealot—give it a try, ask opinions of others, and do some research. Only through education and experience can you learn more about the true nature of things. This is how you develop your skills and knowledge and protect the places you love.

May this book help you on your way to being the consummate outdoorsperson.

Allen O'Bannon

DRESSING AND PACKING FOR THE OUTDOORS

In the backcountry you will see all styles of people. Some folks will be outfitted in Patagucci's latest, while others will be running around in camo (hopefully they're not armed, but in some places you never know). One of the best mountaineers I ever knew used to dress in plaid polyester pants and disco shirts purchased for pennies from a local thrift store. His reasoning was they were made of the same fiber as the fancier stuff, kept him warm, dried quickly, and cost a heck of a lot less. The money he saved on clothes could be used to go climbing. Now, not all of us have the same taste (I personally hate disco) but the fact is there are a number of different ways to do things despite what all the glossy magazine ads (and this book) tell you. Hopefully what you get out of this guide are some general ideas that you can use to create your own reality.

This chapter is all about the systems needed to dress comfortably for the myriad of conditions in the outdoors—plus systems to help you get it all packed. There is no perfect system. You will need to develop your own system that works for you. I am attempting to give you some ideas, but in the end, you need to figure it out for yourself through trial and error. I hope to help you avoid some of the errors.

It takes time to figure out a personalized system of dressing and packing. I started backpacking in the mid-1980s, and I still experiment with different systems, always trying to figure out what works best. My goal is to keep it simple. Strive for simplicity in all you do.

Dressing

To understand the whys of outdoor clothing, you first need to understand the purpose. In the outdoors you have no control over the weather or the temperature. You can't turn up the heat when it gets cold or turn off the wind (I know, I've tried). Clothes, therefore, need to keep you warm when it's cold, block the wind, and keep you dry in the rain. In hot environments like the desert, clothes also serve to protect you from the sun.

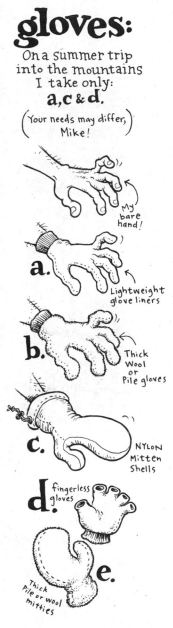

gloves:

On a summer trip into the mountains I take only: **a, c & d.**

(Your needs may differ, Mike!)

My bare hand!

a. Lightweight glove liners

b. Thick Wool or Pile gloves

c. NYLoN Mitten Shells

d. fingerless gloves

e. Thick Pile or wool mitties

In the backcountry it is far more effective to dress in layers of clothing than it is to depend on one do-it-all layer (e.g., an insulated Gore-Tex parka). This allows for more flexibility in what you wear at any one time. Some layers are designed to keep you warm by trapping dead air space. As it gets colder you add more layers and trap more air space. These insulating fabrics include wool, down, and many different types of synthetics. Other layers are made of fabrics that are designed to provide protection from the elements such as the wind or the rain.

Today there are literally hundreds of fabrics to choose from. It would be foolhardy for me (a mere mortal) to try to describe them all. Plus, by the time this is out in print there will probably be another ten new fabrics on the market. I will try to hit on some generalities and leave it to you to do your own market research for your favorite fabric. The emphasis here is on a mountain environment, meaning the clothes you would use in cold and wet weather.

Cotton Leave it at home or at least wear it only on warm, sunny days. Cotton is a hydrophilic fabric, meaning it loves water. Once cotton gets wet it loses its insulating value and will not help keep you warm. It also takes a long time to dry. Personally, I take a maximum of one cotton T-shirt on my trips. If I am going somewhere wet—like the Pacific Northwest—or traveling in the late fall or early spring (when it can be wet and cold almost anywhere you go), I leave all cotton behind.

Synthetics This covers a wide range of materials and is where the major advancements in clothing technology are taking place. Synthetic layers used for warmth can be broken into at least two broad categories: insulating and wicking. Insulating layers are designed to do just that, insulate you from the cold. There are many types of these layers out there ranging from pile to Thinsulate, so take your pick. The advantage of synthetic layers is they insulate when wet and they dry quickly. *Wicking* layers are meant to be worn next to the skin. They work not only to insulate but also to wick water (in the form of sweat) away from your skin, keeping you warmer and drier. There are numerous fabrics out there that claim to be the best at doing this.

Wool The old-fashioned material that just won't quit. Wool comes from sheep. It's a natural fiber that has been around for centuries. Wool seems to go in and out of fashion but currently seems to be on the upswing. Wool also works to insulate you when wet but won't dry as fast as most synthetics. It also tends to be a little heavier. On the positive side though, wool does not get as stinky as most synthetics. This is due to

Dressing and Packing for the Outdoors

the fact that wool fibers have a natural oil in them called lanolin. Lanolin helps to repel dirt and odors, so you may not smell as bad after ten days of bushwhacking (or at least your clothes won't). The higher the quality of wool, the more lanolin it has and the less itchy it will be.

Down The best stuff going for weight-to-warmth ratio. Down is the soft, fluffy stuff that ducks, geese, and other winged creatures use to keep warm. These feathers are actually found underneath the outer feathers we associate with birds. Down is very compressible and durable and makes an excellent insulating material—as long as you don't get it wet. Once wet, it loses all its loft and feels like wet pancake batter sewn into your jacket. It also takes forever to dry. I tend to have the same philosophy about down as I have about cotton. Don't bring too many down layers backpacking and avoid it altogether if the potential exists for a very wet trip. The people who do best with down tend to be anal about their gear, especially about keeping it dry.

What to Take

The type of clothes you take on your trip depends on where you are going and the time of year you are going. So here is some baseline data on which to build.

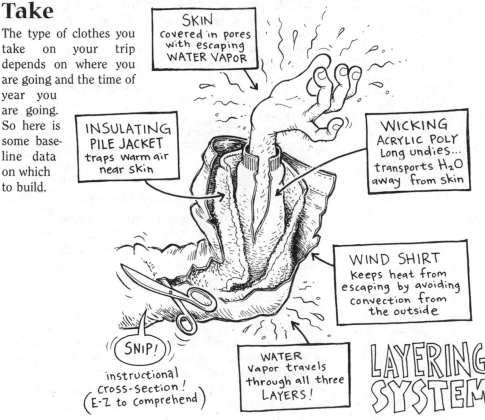

SKIN
covered in pores with escaping WATER VAPOR

INSULATING PILE JACKET
traps warm air near skin

WICKING
ACRYLIC POLY
Long undies...
transports H₂O away from skin

WIND SHIRT
keeps heat from escaping by avoiding convection from the outside

SNIP!
instructional cross-section! (E-Z to comprehend)

WATER
vapor travels through all three LAYERS!

LAYERING SYSTEM

Upper-body insulating layers

Three to four layers is a good rule of thumb depending on the time of year and your ability to produce heat. In the summer I usually get by with three unless I am headed to colder climes like Alaska.

By layers I mean each individual piece of clothing. Insulating layers are just those pieces of clothing meant to trap dead air space such as wool, synthetics, or down. Don't count your rain parka or wind shirt as an insulating layer. I count thin, silk-weight wicking layers as half-layers. Vests are counted as half-layers as well.

One of these layers is always a synthetic wicking layer while the others will be some sort of insulating layer. You also need to know these layers come in different "weights," or thicknesses. The thicker the layer, the warmer it will be. Don't sell yourself short and take three silk-weight layers into the Rocky Mountains. Your pack will be light, but so will you when you leave. Take a combination of clothes and a variety of weights. For myself, I usually go with a lightweight wicking layer, a medium-weight layer such as a wool shirt or "expedition-weight" Capilene (a fabric made by Patagonia; there are other brands that work well too), and then a heavier pile or synthetic fill jacket (the equivalent of Polartec 300). If it is fall, spring, or just a generally colder place, I also add either a mid-weight vest or other mid-weight layer.

It is important that these layers fit over one another. That way you can wear them all at once as well as individually. They should be roomy enough that they help create more dead air space in between each other, but don't bind or constrict you. Test this out before leaving the store and/or heading for the mountains.

Lower-body insulating layers

For your lower body (legs and such) two layers should be enough unless you tend to get cold easily. Lately I have been going with some lightweight Capilene and a pair of light-weight wool dress pants (from my favorite thrift store). Most people prefer some type of mid-weight wicking layer and pile pants. I say have at it; there are plenty of options from expedition-weight under layers to fancy nylon-stretchy pants. The important thing is to have a couple of layers you can put over one another for warmth. One of them needs to be light enough so you don't overheat on those days when it's a little too chilly for shorts but not cold enough for heavy pants. As for shorts, I recommend some type of quick-drying nylon shorts. They're light and don't take up much room in the pack.

ESCAPING BODY HEAT!

I'm c-cold!

(before)

TRAPPED HEAT!

mmm... toasty!

(after!)

IF YOU'RE COLD, PUT ON A HAT!

Head layers

Any type of hat with a brim on it works as a sun hat. The important thing is to be able to stuff it away in your pack, for those times you won't be wearing it. Baseball caps or visors work well. If you find the sun is baking your neck and ears, try wearing a bandanna under the cap to protect them or wear a cap with a 360-degree brim.

In cold weather it is very important to insulate your head. A large amount of heat can be lost through the head, due to all the blood vessels located close to the skin's surface. Don't underestimate the value of a warm hat. Some people I know bring two warm hats they can wear together if it gets really cold. Balaclavas or neck gaiters can also be worn for extra warmth at the neck. There is wisdom in the woodsy adage–"If you're cold, put on a hat."

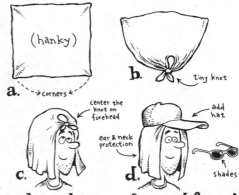

Hanky technique of sun defense!

Worn as directed.

Worn as a hat.

Worn as a neck gaiter.

Worn hood style.

Feet and hands

One pair of gloves (wool or pile) is what I get by with. If you are going to be in snow or if you have poor circulation, you should take mittens and some nylon shells that will fit over them.

Since your feet are so important to what you do, you should bring five pairs of socks with you on any extended trip (three pairs for a weekend outing). Heavy wool or wool/polypropylene blends are the way to go. With five pairs, you can wear

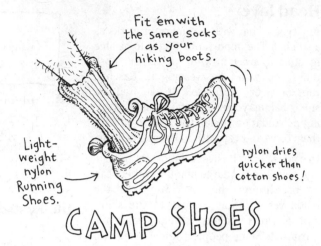

Fit 'em with the same socks as your hiking boots.

Light-weight nylon Running Shoes.

nylon dries quicker than cotton shoes!

CAMP SHOES

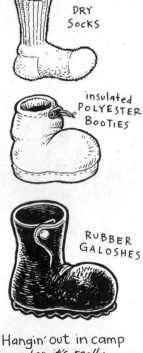

DRY SOCKS

insulated POLYESTER BOOTIES

RUBBER GALOSHES

Hangin' out in camp
when it's really
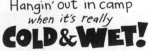
COLD & WET!

two when hiking, have an extra pair to swap with when the others are wet, and keep one pair for wearing around camp and/or for sleeping. I love to hike in two pairs of thick socks, and not for the warmth. Two pairs of socks add a lot of cushioning to your feet, which are taking a pounding out there. It's worth it to provide as much cushioning as you can for those poor little feet—it will pay dividends in the long run for your knees as well.

If wool socks bother your feet, then try adding some nylon liners or use pile socks as an alternative. Different folks have different needs. For some of us, nylon socks cause blisters; for others they are a foot-saver. You will need to experiment to see what works for you.

Neoprene socks are a godsend if you are hiking somewhere with lots of stream crossings, or in a place like Alaska's Brooks Range, where soggy ground is part of the landscape. Neoprene keeps your feet warmer than wool, doesn't absorb as much water (so you won't feel the need to squeeze your socks out after every stream crossing), and will dry quicker. Get as thick a pair as possible.

In addition to boots (covered in the Equipment chapter) you will also want to bring a pair of camp shoes. These can be anything, really. I prefer closed-toed tennis shoes (such as lightweight running shoes) for doing day hikes and such. Some people like to wear sandals. While sandals can be nice for letting your feet air out in camp, they don't offer the protection shoes do. My feet are very important since they are my main form of transportation, so I normally avoid sandals. Shoes offer more protection and warmth in the rain or snow (and from such things as cactus and rocks).

Dressing and Packing for the Outdoors

While not very common, galoshes (like the ones your mom made you wear to school when it was raining) are great for really wet or snowy places. They allow you to keep your foot gear dry when in camp. For people with really bad circulation, a pair of insulated booties worn with galoshes can make a big difference.

Wind layers

When I think of wind gear, I think of something made out of an uncoated lightweight nylon material. It sheds the wind, breathes really well, provides bug protection, and weighs very little. You'll want both a wind shirt and wind pants. If you can find them with pockets all the better, since my guess is you will find yourself wearing these items a lot, and it's nice having your lighter and lip balm handy. Make sure your wind gear fits over all your other layers, rain gear excluded.

Some folks use Gore-Tex or other similar breathable/waterproof fabrics as their wind/rain layer. That's fine, but this has never worked well for me. Maybe I am just too sweaty (I rarely perspire, preferring to just sweat instead), but I get too hot in these fabrics and just wind up wet. I would rather have very breathable wind gear and very waterproof rain gear. But as the lyrics in *Jesus Christ Superstar* go, "I'm just one man," and there are plenty of folks who have good success with waterproof/breathable fabrics.

A simple lightweight **WINDSHIRT** is often superior for hiking in the rain!

Mosquitoes

Yikes! If you are planning a trip to country dominated by these pesky little buggers or their harder hitting cousins, black flies, then you will want to bring some protection. I have survived many trips in bug country (defined as any place where a swat to your back kills at least 25 bugs) with just my wind gear and a mosquito head net. Other options I have seen include jackets

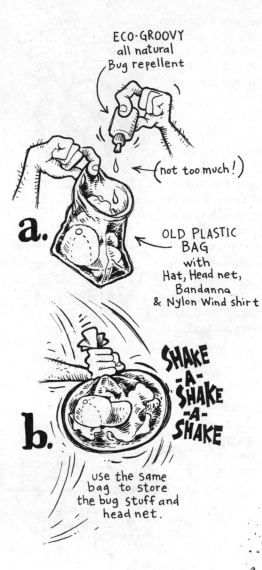

ECO-GROOVY
all natural
Bug repellent

(not too much!)

a.

OLD PLASTIC
BAG
with
Hat, Head net,
Bandanna
& Nylon Wind shirt

b.

SHAKE
-A-
SHAKE
-A-
SHAKE

use the same
bag to store
the bug stuff and
head net.

made out of mosquito netting and netted cotton jackets that are soaked in DEET. Eco-groovy bug dopes like citronella work well, too, and don't eat through plastic pens or have the same environmental implications as DEET—however, they must be applied more often. Personally, I'll stick with wind gear, a head net, and a tiny amount of DEET for those times when I can't wear the head net. This system has worked well even in the buggiest of places.

Rain layers

My favorite piece of rainwear was a knee-length "Sealcoat" jacket made by Patagonia. It was light, relatively dry, and quite fashionable. I wish I had bought more of them before they stopped making them (I only bought two and have almost worn out the second one). Because it had a front zipper it vented really well, which was nice for those times when

wear a hat
with a brim
under a bug head net
when sleeping out
under the stars,
this ain't perfect
but it's better'n nuthin!

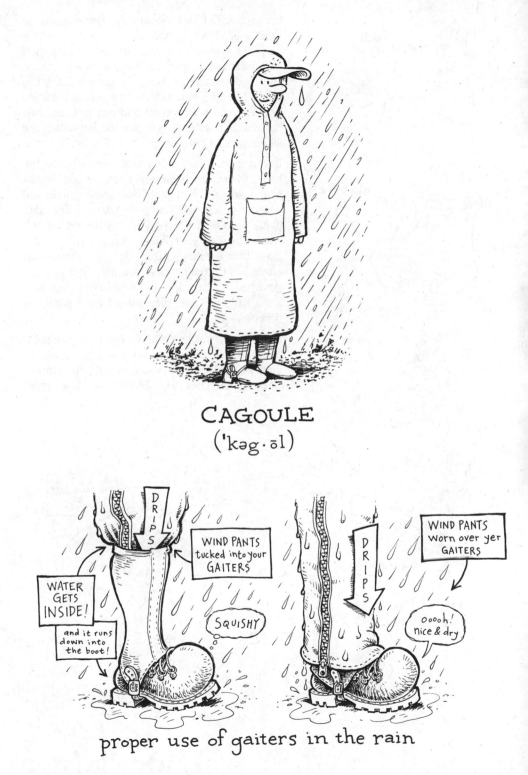

CAGOULE
('kəg·ōl)

proper use of gaiters in the rain

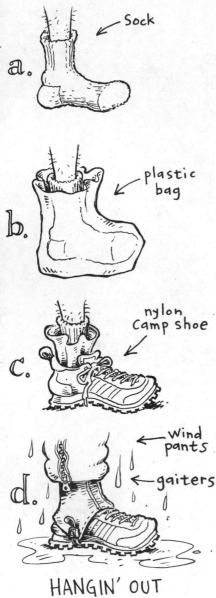

a. Sock

b. plastic bag

c. nylon camp shoe

d. wind pants / gaiters

HANGIN' OUT
in the rain!

the rain wasn't just a downpour. Other pieces of rain gear I have had success with include cagoules (knee-length rain dresses) and rubberized jackets and pants, which, although heavy, are the driest things you can wear, especially the ones lined with cotton to absorb excess perspiration. I would only recommend one of these rubberized rain suits if you plan to be someplace where it rains constantly.

If you have a rain jacket that comes below the knees then you will have no need for rain pants—just wear your wind pants over some gaiters and your lower legs will stay pretty darned dry. Rain pants become a necessity if your jacket doesn't come down to your knees. But if you are in a place that sees only occasional rain showers or afternoon thunderstorms, you may find you can get by with just your wind pants. Your legs may get a little wet but they should have plenty of time to dry.

Don't laugh, but an umbrella can be a nice piece of equipment in places where it rains a lot. As long as it's not too windy, using an umbrella works great. They can't be beat for those times

CAUTION: DON'T POKE any EYES!

Worth the extra weight!

the
Umbrella!
(a luxury item)

SOLAR RADIATION CHECKLIST:

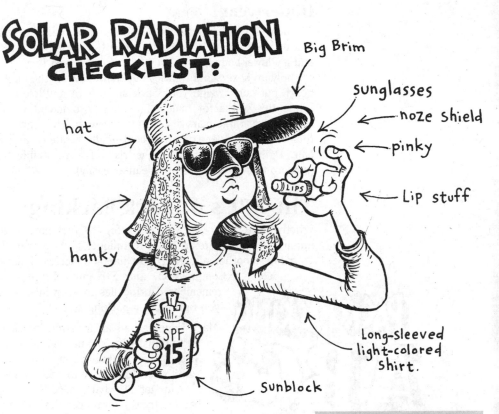

Big Brim

hat

sunglasses

noze shield

pinky

Lip stuff

hanky

Long-sleeved light-colored shirt.

Sunblock

SPF 15

when it is just drizzling on and off. By using the 'brella you can avoid putting on rain gear and stay in your breathable wind gear. You can also create a dry spot under one for cooking.

Desert hiking

Hiking in the desert requires a different mindset when it comes to dressing. If it is the hot time of year, your main concern will not be staying warm but rather staying cool. In this case light-colored cotton long-sleeved, shirts and pants (or shorts) are the way to go. They will be cool, provide protection from the sun (and the prickly plants), and can be wetted down to help increase evaporative cooling. Bring one or two warm synthetic layers in case the nights get cool.

Note: Not all deserts are hot year-round. The coldest I have ever been was during a two-week trip one fall in the canyonlands of Utah, where it never got above freezing.

What do you really need?

When you are deciding what layers to bring, leave behind that just-in-case layer. Be realistic about the weather you'll encounter, and plan for that. Carry only the clothes you'll need to be comfortable in the worst possible conditions— and stick to that! An extra pile jacket is just that, something extra!

Never complain about being cold 'til you are wearing every bit of clothing you brought. If you're still cold, eat. If you're still cold, make camp and get in your sleeping bag.

Underwear

A touchy subject perhaps, but an important one. I normally just go with my nylon shorts (lined with some type of mesh) and my lower-body layers. They seem to work just fine. There are polypro boxers and tighties out there now for the faint of heart, but don't weigh your pack down with multiple pairs. While this works for males, I usually recommend women bring two or three pairs of cotton underwear. They can rinse them out on longer trips and continually rotate in a clean pair. Doing this will lessen the risk of a yeast infection (polypro underwear does not clean as easily).

The ABC's of Pack Packing

Whether you're packing your pack for the first time or the hundredth time, there are a few techniques to make your day go a lot smoother and keep you happier. Access, Balance, Compression, and Streamlined are easily remembered principles to keep in mind as you figure out a packing system.

Mary Poppins had an amazing knack for getting just what she needed out of her bag. While I certainly don't hold a candle to her, I do strive to pack in a way I can get at what's needed without hassle. *Access* to rain gear, extra layers, water, and food all depends on your organization. It's a matter of keeping the stuff you might need during the day handy and knowing where it is so you can find it with ease.

The first thing I do when getting ready to pack is lay everything on the ground around me. That way I can see what I have to pack. I can then triage the things I will need during the day, the things I most likely won't need (but you never know so don't bury them too deeply), and the things I won't need until camp. Examples of stuff to keep close by include sunglasses, sunscreen, extra warm layers, maps, food, and water. If it looks like it might rain, I keep my rain gear handy as well. Otherwise rain gear falls into the category of stuff I may not need—but one never knows. Other things in this

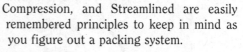

PACK PACKING ABC's

Accessibility **B**alance **C**ompression **S**treamlined

WEIGHT DISTRIBUTED EQUAL SIDE to SIDE and heaviest stuff against your spine (etc.)

NO EMPTY SPACES! (etc.)

water bottle EASY to GET, near the top! (etc.)

EVERYTHING IS INSIDE, nothing to catch on a branch; it's SMooTH! (etc.)

"maybe" category include the rest of my top and bottom layers, and my first-aid kit. Lastly, there are the sleeping bag, extra socks, cooking gear, food, and fuel. These items I bury down deep in the pack because I won't need them until I decide to make camp.

I put small items (toothbrush, floss, knife, etc.) into a stuff sack so they don't get lost in the void of my pack. The top pouch of the pack is a good spot to keep small items, and since it is easily accessible it is a great spot for sunglasses, sunscreen, hats, water bottles, and snack food.

The next principle of pack packing is *balance*. You want to keep heavy items as close to your back as possible. Carrying your pack is easier when the weight is in line with your body, versus out away from it. Also beware of making your pack too top or bottom heavy. Too much weight in the top and the pack takes control, pulling you over. Too much in the bottom and you wind up having to lean forward as you walk to balance it out. Try to get the heaviest items, like food, in that part of your pack that rides at or just below your shoulders. Keep it close to your spine, as well, and think about side-to-side balance. Avoid putting a heavy item on one side of the pack without balancing it out on the other.

The third principle is *compression*. The key here is to really cram things into your pack. No holds barred. Fill up all those dead air spaces in your pack. Stick food into your pot; cram some socks in your tennis shoes. Shove that wind layer into an empty space.

ON TRAIL:
position the weight against the spine between your shoulder blades

OFF TRAIL:
Position the weight lower against the Spine above the small of your back.

WEIGHT TOO HIGH!
and You'll feel tippy & out of BALANCE!

WEIGHT TOO LOW,
and You'll need to hunker forward to keep it centered above your hips

The BOUNCE method of pack compression:

* PLEASE REMEMBER ... don't pack your camera 'til AFTER the bouncing!

It's the greenhorn that attaches
everything to the outside of his pack!

PUT IT INSIDE!

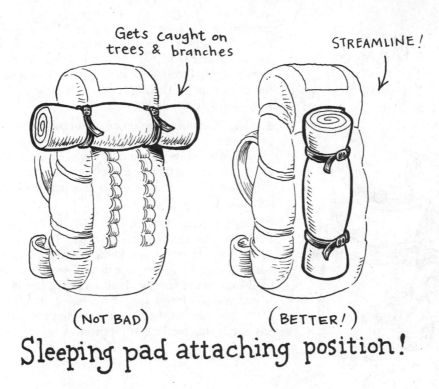

Gets caught on trees & branches

STREAMLINE!

(NOT BAD)   (BETTER!)

Sleeping pad attaching position!

Packing a pack is an art, and a well-packed pack looks solid from the outside, no dimples or bulges showing where the fry pan or some such item is or isn't. Your pack should look like it did in the shop when it was stuffed with all that cotton wadding. This allows you to fit everything inside your pack and avoid the syndrome of having the pack look like there is more strapped to the outside than there is packed inside.

Which brings me to our last principle—*streamlined.* Now maybe I am just finicky, but I like to get as much stuff in my pack as possible and avoid strapping stuff to the outside. This includes my sleeping pad, which I often roll up, stick in the pack first, and then unroll so it makes an empty tube inside the pack. I then pack everything inside this tube. You need a big pack to do this, but it has the advantage of weather proofing your pack because water will run down the outside of your pad instead of penetrating deeper into the

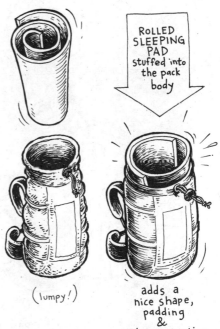

ROLLED SLEEPING PAD stuffed into the pack body

(lumpy!)

adds a nice shape, padding & water protection

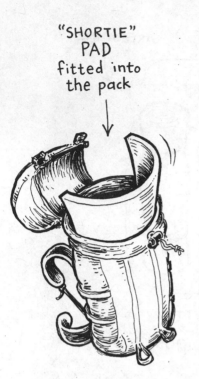

"SHORTIE"
PAD
fitted into
the pack

contents of the pack. My theory is, if it's in your pack, it's less likely to get lost, wet, or broken. This may not matter much on a trail, but if you are ever bushwhacking through the brush, you will soon see the advantage to this. Plus it's high style to be streamlined. It just looks good.

Anything that does wind up on the outside of your pack needs to be well attached. I have picked up more than a few items, typically shoes, off the trail. Don't just strap it down, tie it off to something, so if it does slip out from under a strap, it's still attached.

The biggest secret to pack packing is getting your own little personal system down pat. This allows you to pack faster as you know where each item goes. No longer will you have to lay everything out on the ground in the rain. It also makes it less likely that you will forget something. Listed are a few tricks that have worked well for me, but everyone has a style that works best for them.

SLEEPING
BAG
compression
stuff sack

SLEEPING
BAG
just tossed in

PRE-LINE
your pack with
a trash bag

a tricky
shape for packing.

easily smooshed
and compacted
sleeping bag.

- Try packing your pack as one big potato sack—shove it all in from the top. This way you can really cram stuff in without having to go to war with a zipper in order to close it.

TIE OFF the CORD LOCK

COMPRESSION STUFF SACK packed LOUSY!

NICE!

- Put the sleeping bag in first. You won't need it till camp, and as a large bulky item, it fills up a lot of space, helping you avoid a bottom-heavy pack.

- Pack the sleeping bag in a compression stuff sack along with a pair of socks. This way you will always have something warm and dry to stick over your toes without having to search the socks out before bed. If you are in a wet place, line your compression sack with a trash bag before stuffing the sleeping bag. Mike likes to stuff his sleeping bag right into the pack. This works as long as your bag isn't too bulky and the entire pack is lined with a garbage bag.

the same pack:

- Next cram as much stuff around the sleeping bag as possible. This could include things like camp shoes, the tent, ground cloth, or bivy sack. It depends a lot on what the weather is like. For example, pack the tent last if it's raining. That way it is the last thing down and the first thing up, meaning you will spend less time in the rain. If the weather's nice, however, bury it down deep.

PACKED
using multiple stuff sacks.

PACKED
without any stuff sacks, just cramming it all in!

- Pack the tent body, rain fly, and poles separately. This allows you to stuff them around things instead of having to stuff things around them.

important:

NO EMPTY SPACES!
(when you're packing!)

• Don't use too many stuff sacks. Not only do they add up to a lot of weight but it's much easier to cram individual items around something if they're not balled up in a stuff sack.

• Pack the fuel bottle upright and below the food. This will help ensure that you don't accidentally leak gas on the food. Down alongside the sleeping bag works well. An outside pocket will also work, but the bottle is more likely to get dinged up.

Keeping it light

Weight is the enemy of the backpacker. Believe me, it's no fun carrying a 100-pound pack. When I was young and dumb my friends and I used to take pride in carrying all we could on our backs. A cast iron skillet was just the thing for making pancakes. Luckily I survived that phase and am now a proponent of going as light as possible.

There are some good reasons to go out with less. First, you're going to spend a lot of time with that beast on your back so you might as well enjoy those long hours on the trail. The act of moving through the wilderness can be a time of joy in a beautiful place, or it can be a miserable grunt with all your effort focused on getting to camp so you can rid yourself of that behemoth. With a light pack, you'll cover more miles, quicker, and have extra energy when you get to your campsite. Second, it's the skilled camper who can do more with less, and this is a real point of pride. Plus, you just plain need to keep track of less stuff! Finally, your knees and ankles take enough of a beating, so be nice to them. You are much less likely to injure yourself going light— simple strains and sprains end too many outings. Knee surgery shouldn't be part of your camping experience!

Separate your needs from your wants. Most of the weight in a pack comes because you have some nifty little item you saw somewhere. In reality, you probably don't need that item. Desire has a way of convincing us we need something that could be done without.

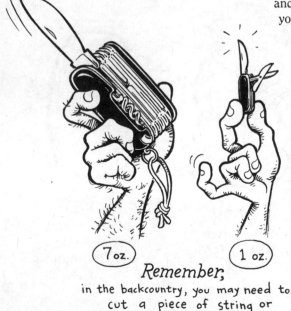

7 oz.   1 oz.

Remember,
in the backcountry, you may need to cut a piece of string or trim some moleskin...

Think: "Would I be okay if I didn't have this?" Keep the first-aid kit, leave the folding chair. Scrutinize everything! Use a little kitchen scale and weigh everything. Fill your pack and weigh it, pull out those "maybe" items, and weigh it again. At most allow yourself one luxury item. Mine is usually a book.

Ounces add up to pounds and pounds add up to pain. However, you can't take a 60-pound pack and pull out one unnecessary item to make it a 50-pound pack. It doesn't work that way. It is only by getting rid of a bunch of smaller items (ounces) that you start to shave off the pounds. Drop stuff sacks; leave behind the cotton T-shirt and the candle lantern. Some people even go so far as to cut their toothbrush in half or take all the little strings off the tea bags.

I rarely, if ever, go out with a pack that is over 60 pounds, and that includes climbing gear and eight days' worth of food. Most of the time I keep my pack closer to a nice 50 pounds

REPAIR KIT ESENTIAL!

DUCT TAPE
WRAPPED
AROUND
A PENCIL

fix sumpthin'
&
write a note!

Some tips on keeping it light:

- Make going light the centerpiece of your trip and design everything around this. Get the entire team to work toward this goal. One tube of toothpaste in the group is fine.

- Can you substitute something lighter or more multi-purpose for any given item? Take only a tiny knife, not a gigantic one. Maybe you don't even need a knife. Can you drink tea out of your water bottle? Do you truly need a mug? Really think about everything and its purpose. Be creative.

- Realize that an inflatable sleeping pad is heavier than an Ensolite foam pad. This is where a scale can really be enlightening.

- Remove packaging from everything! Food, film, batteries . . . get rid of it.

- Eat everything you bring. This needs to be part of the big plan. Finish the last of the food before reaching the trailhead.

- Bring a light-weight tarp or rain fly instead of a tent.

- By sleeping in your layers you can use a lighter-weight sleeping bag (and it makes getting up on those chilly mornings a lot easier).

- Plastic soda bottles are lighter than hi-tech water bottles and virtually indestructible.

- Your cup and bowl can be one and the same.

- Iodine tablets weigh a micro-fraction of the lightest-weight water filter.

- Be efficient when you use the stove so you can carry less fuel.

- Actively challenge that little voice that says: "But I've always taken that."

- Challenge your partner to come up with a lighter pack than you or try to beat your previous low pack-weight record.

- Ask some low-weight fanatics for ideas. This can be a passionate subject and it might be hard to shut 'em up.

Things to leave behind:

- Cotton T-shirt

- Huge bottles of sun block, industrial-sized toothpaste tubes, moisturizer (your skin will get oily all by itself), giant bottles of soap, etc.

- Camp chairs—learn to sit on the ground.

- Big knives, big binoculars, Walkmans, radios, cell phones, GPS units.

- Truckloads of camera gear. There are some amazing, high-quality little point and shoots, inexpensive and light.

- Big books you'll never read.

- Overly huge first-aid kits, repair kits, and sewing kits. You need these items, but be realistic about what's prudent and what's overkill.

or so for the same length trip. As a general guide, you should shoot for a pack weight of less than 40 percent of your body weight. This gets tough on extended trips (seven or more days) when food weight really begins to add up.

Ray Jardine, the guru of lightweight trips, has done many thousands of miles with a pack that weighs under 9 pounds, excluding food and water. While this may seem extreme, it's all about having a system and a way of doing things that accomplish your goals.

Keeping it all dry

Water is a very heavy item. A quart of water weighs about 2 pounds. A backpack full of water would be impossible to lift. For this reason alone it is worth knowing some strategies to waterproof your pack. Luckily there are lots of different options, and they are all relatively simple. You can use your Ensolite pad, as discussed earlier, to keep water from penetrating

KEEP TENTS and SLEEPING BAGS clean and dry while packing by using your SHOULDER to keep 'em off the ground!

line it with a plastic GARBAGE BAG!

PACK YOUR SLEEPING BAG FEET FIRST!

PACK or COMPRESSION STUFF SACK

WATERPROOFING your PACK

Line the Pack with a big plastic **GARBAGE BAG** — approx 25¢ —

store-bought **PACK COVER** — approx $25⁰⁰ —

CONTRACTOR BAGS work great!
(3-mil, 45-gallon size)
Find 'em at a Hardware store

beyond the material of your pack. Lining the pack with a heavy-duty plastic trash bag (look for contractor bags in the hardware store) will serve the same purpose, with the added advantage of being able to use it over your pack at night. You do need to be careful not to rip it when packing, however. These are the options I get by with in most of the places I go hiking—they add very little extra weight (the ensolite method requires nothing extra at all). The only disadvantage to these methods is that the pack material gets wet. This dries quickly though, the next time the sun pops out.

If I am going someplace where lots of rain is more common than not, I will consider taking a store-bought pack cover. They keep the entire pack dry, unless you drop it in a river. However, they add about a pound to the pack's weight (remember, it all adds up), so they are really only worth it if they are keeping a pint of rain from soaking into the pack material day after day.

EQUIPMENT

The right gear can make or break a trip, and while I'll always have a great respect for those hardy souls who make do with whatever is at hand, let's face it, life is easier with the right stuff. But just what is the right stuff? What one person always considers to be an essential is a luxury by somebody else's standards. The answer, of course, is that you need to decide for yourself what is important and what is not. Mike and I will give you some guidelines for what works. Don't expect 100 percent agreement from us though; we are just as opinionated as everyone else when it comes to our own gear and that means we disagree plenty, but we'll do our best to put you on the right track.

Some thoughts on gear: Keep it simple. If it has lots of bells and whistles then it also has more to go wrong. I like gear that is simple, durable, and easy to repair. It may not be as appealing to the eye, but it's not my eyes I'm worried about. I like stuff that is easy to take care of and will take all the abuse a long trip is going to inflict. Some people love to dink around with equipment, endlessly modifying and/or cleaning it. Me, I want my gear to take care of itself, and hopefully, me along with it. Weight is what I worry about next, especially now that my bones tend to creak more then they used to. Keep it light. This will enable you to travel farther and faster, leaving you more time to enjoy the place you're traveling to. Of course the easiest way to save weight is to leave out all the nonessentials and take only what you truly need for survival. But more on my biases later.

Backpacks

Along with the boots on your feet, your backpack affects how you enjoy each hiking day. A badly fitting pack is miserable. It takes all the joy out of hiking. So take your time in choosing a pack and get one that is comfortable to carry and easy to pack. A well-fitting pack places most of the weight on your hips. Only about 20 percent of the weight should come to rest on your shoulders when the hip belt is tightened down on your waist. The pack should move when you move and not sway back and forth.

It can be overwhelming to walk into a store and be confronted with anywhere between ten and twenty backpacks to choose from. It usually makes me want to walk

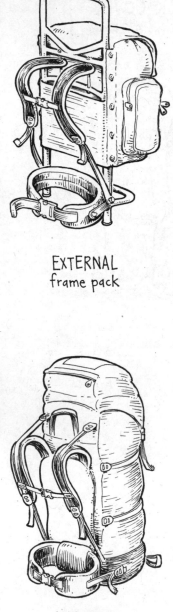

EXTERNAL
frame pack

INTERNAL
frame pack

Most packs have a simple size adjustment to match the LENGTH of your BACK

out of the store, since I'm not used to so much sensory overload. But if you need a pack there's only one way to get one, and that's to plow through them all and find the one that meets your needs and fits well. Talk to different people to see what packs they like. Get the salespeople to fit you up with a couple of different packs, and make sure they put some weight in them—that way you can see how they ride on your hips and shoulders. Don't just buy the first one that hits your fancy; take your time selecting a pack so you get one that fits your body and needs well.

There are two basic types of packs: internal frame and external frame. Internal frame packs are also called soft packs in some places. An external frame pack may simply be referred to as a frame pack. If you mostly plan to hike on-trail and prefer not to spend a lot of money on a pack, then an external frame pack is probably the way to go. They carry weight well, tend to not be as expensive as a soft, internal frame pack (although this depends on the pack), and are easier to pack. But if you plan to hike off-trail a lot, or want the current in high fashion, then go with a soft pack. By design, an internal frame pack carries the weight closer to your back, which improves your balance in uneven terrain. They are also less likely to get tangled in the brush, if you happen to enjoy bushwhacking in places like the Pacific Northwest.

Now no matter what type of pack you choose, there are a few things to keep in mind. One is simplicity. Avoid packs with too many bells and whistles. Not only do these things add up to more weight and more money, but, as I said before, there is more to go wrong. I like packs that are streamlined in shape, don't have a lot of zippers (and the zippers they do

How big is a big pack?

For an expedition longer than eight days you should get an internal frame pack of no less then 6,000 cubic inches (95 liters).

An external frame pack should be at least 3,500 cubic inches (55 liters) with room to strap a sleeping bag on at the bottom and with an extension bar at the top for strapping on extra stuff.

If you are inclined toward smaller packs, then you can always add on side pockets for longer trips. I know lots of people who use this system because they like the pockets for organizing things. However, if you plan to do lots of bushwhacking, I think you'll discover pockets are more of a pain because they get hung up in heavy brush.

candle lantern

(HEAVY, EXPENSIVE and BREAKABLE!)

old plastic bag

Sand!

(cheap, light & WORKS GREAT!)

have should be beefy), and pack from the top down. I am not a big fan of divided packs. While at first they may seem easier to pack than a top-loader, with some practice, a top-loader is far simpler to pack. (Don't be afraid to slice the divider out with a razor if this is the only type of pack you can find or the only one that seems to fit right.) In addition to this, divided packs by their nature have more zippers, and zippers are usually the first thing to break on a pack. Weight is another consideration—the heavier the pack, the more weight you will ultimately have on your back. On the other hand, if a pack is made with material that is too light, it probably won't last long unless you treat it gently. I like packs that are made with a durable material but are simple enough in design they remain light.

Lastly, I like large packs that compress well. While a large pack will weigh more than a smaller one, it is more versatile. Unless you are the type of person who likes to collect things, you probably won't own more than one pack (day pack excluded). A large pack gives you room to expand. If you are doing short trips, then you can put everything inside it and carry nothing on the outside, but you'll also have the option of doing longer trips if the desire ever strikes you.

BIG Stuff Sack!

sew 'em on

1 1/2-inch webbing

little 3/4-inch Fastex buckles

3/4-inch webbing

Easy Homemade lightweight day pack!

Day packs

I have had lots of luck sewing a pair of lightweight shoulder straps onto an extra-large stuff sack to use as a lightweight day pack. It is a simple solution to carrying around a heavier day pack. Of course you can always just compress your internal frame pack and use it as a day pack. Leaving the lid behind lightens it up even more.

Sleeping Bags

Three-season bags are often the hardest thing to decide on. Do you want one for warm summers or the colder seasons of fall and spring? Also, where are you planning on going? The mountains will require a

GOOD NEWS! FART SMELLS can't escape from your lofty & puffy sleepin' bag!

mmmm...

warmer bag than the desert. Your best bet, other than buying multiple bags, is to get one that works for the season and place where you plan to do most of your camping. If you find yourself in a warmer place, you can sleep with the zipper open. A colder situation can be dealt with by wearing a hat to bed, more clothes, and/or putting more insulation between you and the ground.

As to the type of bag you get, there are literally thousands of choices. I recommend staying away from any bag that has cowboys or ducks printed on the inside unless all you are planning to do is car camp. For backpacking you are looking for a mummy bag of some type (vs. a rectangular bag) filled with either a synthetic material or down.

Down

Down is the insulating feathers of either ducks or geese. The higher quality the down, the better its insulating value. There is nothing like a down bag for stuffing in your pack—it weighs so little and stuffs so small. As of yet there is no synthetic material (although some are getting close) that will beat down for its weight-to-warmth ratio. On the other hand, there is nothing as horrible as a wet down sleeping bag. It no longer insulates and takes forever to dry. If you plan on buying a down bag you need to be totally committed to keeping it dry. If you plan to go camping someplace wet, consider a synthetic bag.

Beddie Bye!

HOOD
HAT
WELL FED!
GLOVES
lightweight SUMMER BAG
DRY SOX

(Save some weight)

Carry a
LIGHTWEIGHT
sleeping bag
and
WEAR **ALL** YOUR
CLOTHES to BED!

Synthetic materials

Synthetic materials are just different forms of polyester. Common fills found in sleeping bags include Quallofil, Hollofil, and Polarguard, although there are more on the way I'm sure. The biggest and most important thing to remember about synthetic bags is they still retain their insulating value when wet—unlike down. A synthetic bag will also dry at least four times as fast as a down bag. For these two reasons alone most people choose to go with a synthetic bag. Another advantage is that synthetic bags tend to be less expensive. The main disadvantage to synthetic bags lies in their compressibility (or lack of) and extra weight. While some types of synthetics are approaching down in this realm, none of them can truly compete with down yet. This is especially true when you factor in durability. Synthetics bags tend to break down and lose their loft faster then a feather bag.

So what is loft? Well in general, loft is the measurement of the bag's height when it is lying flat on the ground. The more loft, the more dead air space and the warmer the bag. Bags of equal loft will be equally warm, even if the insulation is different. A thin bag will be less warm than one that is fluffy, no matter what the temperature rating of the bag says—something to keep in mind if you are thinking about buying a used bag.

Most companies will give a temperature rating for the bags they make. This is a good way to get a sense for the type of bag you want and is also useful for comparison between bags. Be careful about how you interpret the rating system, though. A 20-degree (Fahrenheit) bag may not keep you warm if it's 20 degrees out. It depends on your metabolism more than anything. It is just a useful guide. If you are a cold sleeper, then you should consider getting a bag with more loft (and a lower temperature rating) than if you are a warm sleeper.

The design of a bag is just as important as its rating. A bag

Hmmm... Fascinating!

measuring sleeping bag loft

with a draft collar is warmer than one without
because it traps air better, keeping the warm
air inside. A roomier bag is harder to warm
up than a tight-fitting one
because there is more space
to heat. Bags with a draft flap
behind the zipper will trap air
more effectively than ones
without.

I use a 20-degree bag for most of my
summer camping. I am a warm sleeper
and rarely get cold. I also do most of my
camping in the mountains where temperatures are cooler. If you are camping
in the desert during the summer, I recommend a lighter-weight bag. Fall and
early spring campers should consider
warmer bags. Remember this is just my
guideline. You should do some research
about the average temperatures in the
places you plan to go, and try out a friend's
bag to get a sense for what works for you.

Draft collar

Zipper draft flap

Cord lock for scrunchin' the face hole smaller.

Sleeping Pads and Bivy Bags

Sleeping pads do more than just cushion you from the hard
ground. Their main purpose is to insulate you from the
ground and help you sleep warmer. For this reason you are
looking for some type of closed-cell foam pad like Ensolite or
Evasote. Open-cell foam may be cushy but does not provide
much insulation by itself since the open cells do not trap air
(creating dead air space). Some people supplement their

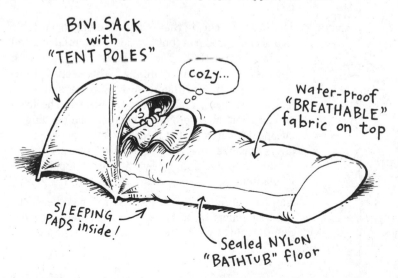

BIVI SACK with "TENT POLES"

cozy...

Water-proof "BREATHABLE" fabric on top

SLEEPING PADS inside!

Sealed NYLON "BATHTUB" floor

MORE!

OVERINFLATING
will create more leaks
and
it'll be a rock-hard
sleeping surface!

hmmm...
comfy!

RELEASE some AIR;
it may feel too soft,
but
it'll firm up when you
lie on it!

pfff...

this is
LITTER!

ENSOLITE FOAM PAD
carried on the
outside of your pack
showing
BUSHWHACKING DAMAGE!

Use a
Stuff sack
or...
PUT IT INSIDE
your pack!

closed-cell pad with a small (2 feet by 4 feet) piece of 2-inch thick "egg-crate" style open-cell foam, which can be found in the bedding department at Kmart and purchased for a few bucks. The weight of this small extra pad is negligible, but it can add a lot of comfort in the shoulder-to-hip area when sleeping. For packing, it can be rolled right up inside your closed-cell pad.

Another good choice that is slightly more comfortable than a closed-cell pad (but heavier) is an inflatable pad like a Therm-a-Rest. Therm-a-Rests are filled with open-cell foam that you "inflate." This keeps convective air cells from forming, so the air stays more or less in one place, creating dead air space. The foam and air combine to provide insulation and padding. A cheapo air mattress that is just air space between two layers of rubber may be comfortable, but since the air is allowed to circulate freely, they don't supply much insulation.

Bivy bags are just Gore-Tex sacks or some other material that claims to be breathable yet waterproof. You pull them over your sleeping bag for extra protection

against the elements or for bivouacs without a tent. The newer they are, the better job they do at shedding the rain. They also add about 10 degrees of additional warmth to your sleeping bag, especially in windy conditions. I like a simple light-weight nylon one for keeping the dew off my bag when I sleep out. That way I can pack my bag without having to wait for the dew to dry off. Some companies make them even fancier (and heavier) by adding poles to them and such.

In terms of ground cloths, I rarely use one. I don't see the need for them unless you are in an area with soggy wet ground or you want something to keep you off the dirt or sand. It's a free world.

Boots

When you're out backpacking you quickly realize how important your feet are. Without them you literally wouldn't be backpacking! Finding a comfortable pair of boots is perhaps the most important part of the hiking experience. One of my most painful memories is of hiking off Mount Kenya in Africa with blisters the size of half-dollars on my heels. I cringed with every step. I had to force myself to walk to the trailhead. Believe me, it's worth taking the time and paying the money to get a good-fitting boot.

If you plan on doing long trips with lots of weight in your pack, then get a sturdy pair of boots with full leather uppers

BOOT & PACK CHART

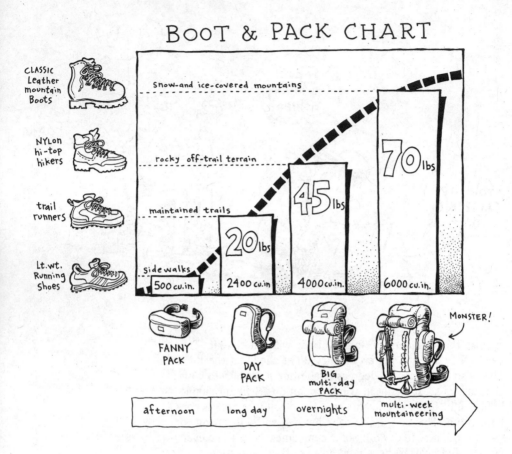

CLASSIC Leather mountain Boots

NYLon hi-top hikers

trail runners

Lt.wt. Running Shoes

Snow-and ice-covered mountains

rocky off-trail terrain

maintained trails

sidewalks

70 lbs

45 lbs

20 lbs

500 cu.in.

2400 cu.in.

4000 cu.in.

6000 cu.in.

MONSTER!

FANNY PACK

DAY PACK

BIG multi-day PACK

afternoon | long day | overnights | multi-week mountaineering

HEY! this is **NOT** a carrying loop!

that offer lots of support. For doing a lot of off-trail travel, sturdy boots are especially important. Not only do these boots offer good ankle support (so you don't sprain your ankle), but they also protect your feet from the abuse that comes with travel on uneven terrain. In today's techno world, boots no longer have to weigh 5 pounds each to be considered sturdy. The saying that "a pound on the foot is like 5 on the back" actually has a lot of truth to it. Just think of how many steps you take and how many times you are lifting that extra weight. On short trips with a light pack, lightweight hiking shoes (basically beefed-up hightops) may be the way to go. Especially if you have strong ankles and aren't a klutz like me. You need to be careful if you choose to go with lightweight hikers though—you don't want to pay the price of a twisted ankle. Lightweight hikers also won't stand up to as much abuse as quality leather boots, so be prepared to replace them more often. In terms of price, with boots you usually get what you pay for.

Take your time finding boots, and try a few pairs. Boots, like feet, come in all shapes and sizes. The only way to know how they fit is to walk around in them. Wear as many socks as you plan to hike in (I like to wear two pairs) when fitting boots. It is also a good idea to try them on in the afternoon, when your feet are bigger due to swelling.

While you want to lace the boots snugly, you should avoid cranking them down so hard that your fingers blister. In a proper-fitting boot, you should feel a little heel lift, but no more than about an eighth of an inch. Kick something (but not your cat) solid. If your toe hits the front of the boot on the first or second kick, then they are too small and walking downhill will be torture. Your toe should nudge up against the front of the boot on the third or fourth kick. Lots of retail stores now have a little ramp you can walk down to see if your toes hit the front of the boot. If you can, walk around the store and do some other browsing with the boots on. The more time you can spend in the boots, the more your feet can tell you about the fit. They should feel comfortable without any pressure points. The heavier the boot, the more important it is to walk around. Good quality leather boots don't feel like tennis shoes, and it takes time to adjust.

Simple WEBBING handle

Handy source of BACKCOUNTRY DUCT TAPE!

After purchasing your boots take some time to waterproof them. Most boots come with suggestions on how to do this. If not, then the procedure is to take beeswax, or some other commercially available sealant, and rub it into the leather. Let the boots sit in a warm place for a few hours and repeat after the

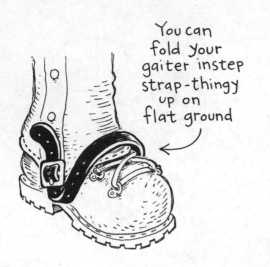

You can
fold your
gaiter instep
strap-thingy
up on
flat ground

a little
key-chain ring
is a better
solution for
the gaiter's
laces hook

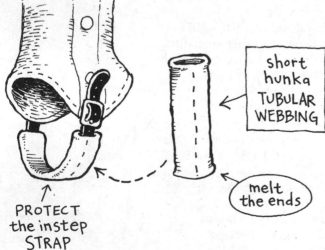

short
hunka
TUBULAR
WEBBING

melt
the ends

PROTECT
the instep
STRAP

Equipment

sealant has soaked in. I try to get three or four layers on my boots before a trip.

Gaiters

Most folks use gaiters only when snow is on the ground. And for weekend hikes this is fine. However, gaiters are much more multipurpose than people think. For one, on long trips they are invaluable for keeping your feet and socks clean. By wearing gaiters on dusty or sandy trails you keep dirt and such out of your boots. Cleaner socks and feet equal fewer blister problems.

Additionally, gaiters can help keep your feet drier during quick shallow-stream crossings. In rainy conditions they help shed water to the outside of the boot rather than funneling it into the boot. Short, lightweight gaiters, called puttees, are great for places where your main concern is keeping grit out of the boots. Beefier gaiters do a better job at keeping feet dry in wet conditions—although nothing will stop them from getting wet eventually.

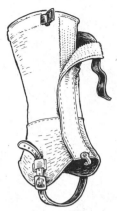

modern velcro
GAITER

Eating Utensils and Cooking Gear

Let's keep this simple—everyone has their own personal choice about what they like to eat with. I find a spoon and a bowl is all I ever need. My bowl is also my cup, or is it the other way around? Doesn't really matter; what matters is I have something that holds food and/or a hot drink. Most people prefer both a cup and a bowl, but a water bottle holds a cup of hot tea just fine when your bowl is occupied. In cold weather you can stick that hot bottle in your parka when you're not drinking from it. Try that with an insulated mug!

As long as you're not eating salads, you'll find a spoon is fine for moving food from your bowl to your mouth. A fork is just excess weight. Knives are useful for slicing things (including fingers, so be careful!), but there is no need to bring one of those big survival knives—something small and light will work just fine. Multipurpose units like a Swiss Army knife or a Leatherman have their uses, but don't go overboard here either. It's rare that I ever have a use for more than my spoon.

In terms of cook gear, I am all for going light and simple. A pot, a fry pan, and a spatula will keep me pretty happy. Take a pot that will hold just the amount of water needed to make a hot drink for you and your friends and/or hold enough pasta to stave off hunger (2 to 3 quarts). If the pot doesn't

NO MUG!

mmm!

HOT TEA!

hand warmer

The humble
WATER BOTTLE
is a superior
alternative
to
carrying a mug!

lightweight COOK SYSTEM
(complete!)

heavyweight COOK SYSTEM
(overly complete!)

have a handle, then you will also need some pot grips. A fry pan with a nonstick surface is nice, and if you like bread products it should be thick enough to evenly distribute the heat (this keeps things from burning). Bring a lid that will fit both the fry pan and your pot.

Stoves

With so many of us humans taking to the backcountry, cooking on fires has gone out of vogue. And for good reason: it's simply too much impact on the land. Stoves are now an essential piece of equipment.

Butane, white gas, plate burner versus port burner—what does it all mean? Well, let me try to sort it out. Butane, propane, or cartridge stoves burn fuel that vaporizes naturally in our atmosphere. Because of this you can turn on the valve and light them. White gas or liquid fuel stoves need to be primed, or heated up, to vaporize the gas before they will burn properly. Although at a disadvantage because of the

BUTANE STOVE

increased time and trouble to prime them, liquid fuel stoves burn hotter, are less costly to buy fuel for, and don't require as much packaging since you don't need to buy a new cartridge each time. In addition, cartridge-type stoves don't work as well in cold temps whereas white gas stoves will work just fine. Therefore white gas is probably the way to go for most campers. Those folks who plan to avoid cold-weather camping and instead stick to mostly short two- to three-day trips may want to consider a butane or propane stove for ease of operation.

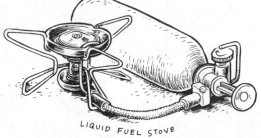

LIQUID FUEL STOVE

Stoves with a plate burner such as MSR's XGK burn loud and hot. The roar produced by them is comforting to some but tends to make conversation difficult. Stoves with ported burners (Coleman's Peak 1 for example) are much quieter and, although they may not boil a pot of water as fast, what's a few seconds compared to a stove that sounds like a jet taking off?

Another important feature to look for in stoves is ease of repair. There's nothing like having to take a stove apart when all you want is a hot drink. For this reason I like a stove with as few parts as possible. I will take a risk here and say that my favorite stove of all time is the MSR WhisperLite. It is a simple stove that is light, compact, and dependable. It does have its idiosyncrasies, but don't we all? As for those critics who say that these stoves don't simmer well, I will answer; the key to getting any stove to simmer well, is to not over-pressurize it when using the pump. But there are lots of choices out there, so look around for the stove that suits you best.

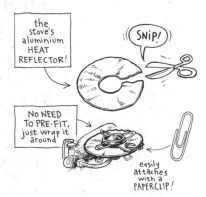

the stove's aluminium HEAT REFLECTOR!

((SNIP!))

No NEED TO PRE-FIT, just wrap it around

easily attaches with a PAPERCLIP!

TARP!

easily
SLEEPS 3!

size: 8ft × 10ft
weight: (1 lb. 8oz.)
cost: about 30 bucks!

takes 20 minutes to set up

TENT
barely
SLEEPS 3

weight: about 9 lbs.
cost: about $400⁰⁰

takes about 20 minutes
to set up

Shelters

There are two basic types of shelters used for backpacking and infinite variations of each. One of your first decisions will be whether to use a tent or a tarp. There are advantages and disadvantages to each.

Tarps

Tarps have the main advantage of being cheap and light. In fact there is no contest here. While tarps take a little more skill to set up, when done right they are just as dry and comfy as a tent. In fact, they may even be drier since you get more air circulation under a tarp than you do in a tent. Which leads to another advantage—it is far safer and easier to cook under a tarp. No carbon monoxide danger to worry about, no need to worry about spilled water in the tent, and less chance of setting the whole place on fire. Of course in bear country this advantage goes right down the drain, as you need to cook far away from where you plan to sleep anyway. In fact, tents are a better idea if you plan to camp in areas frequented by grizzlies. Tents do a better job of camouflaging you as a possible meal or threat. A tarp doesn't keep bugs out, so if the areas you are going to have more than their fair share of creepy crawly things or flying bloodsuckers, consider a shelter that offers a bug net. Your sanity may depend on it.

There are many types of tarps out there, from single sheets of nylon you can pitch like an A-frame between trees, to pyramid-shaped shelters that offer more protection from the wind. I have always been a fan of tarps because of their simplicity, weight, and price.

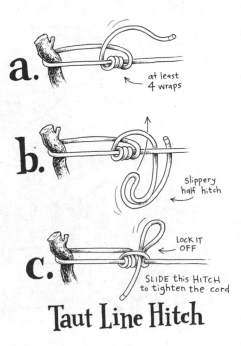

a. ← at least 4 wraps

b. slippery half hitch

c. LOCK IT OFF ← SLIDE this HITCH to tighten the cord

Taut Line Hitch

Tents

Tents are nice for getting out of the environment around you. Maybe it's the bugs or the sand, the wind or the endless rain, but whatever the case, tents provide an enclosed shelter to ward off the offending environment. In areas devoid of trees, tents are advantageous because you don't need a tree to set them up and they shed wind better than most tarps.

Look for simplicity of design and ease of setup in a tent. If it's easier to solve the Gordian knot than to set up the tent, get something else. Tents come in all shapes and sizes, and not all are created equal. The more poles a tent has, the more it will weigh, and the more fussing you will have to do to set it up. A vestibule gives you a place to store gear but also adds weight and may make getting in and out harder. Cheap zippers won't last long, nor will a cheap tent.

Some tents are freestanding, meaning they set up without any stakes or guy lines. Of course, you still need to stake these tents out if you don't want them to blow away. Other tents need to be staked out in order to be fully set up. I have used both kinds and don't see any advantages or disadvantages to either. They're just different.

Single-walled tents are light and easy to set up but more expensive and not as dry as double-walled tents. Single-walled

the important GAP BETWEEN the two LAYERS!

RAIN FLY made of waterproof NYLON

Moisture H₂O Vapor

amazing ARCHITECTURAL cross-section!

DOUBLE-WALLED TENT

Allen & Mike's Really Cool Backcountry Ski Book!

TENT BODY made of "breathable" NYLON

"BATH TUB" bottom of waterproof NYLON on the tent body

tents attempt to breathe by using a waterproof, breathable material akin to Gore-Tex. They work best in the snow, but I have successfully used one in very rainy conditions. Double-walled tents are designed to breathe, thereby lessening the amount of condensation that forms on the inside. A double-walled tent uses an inside body (the tent body) of very breathable nylon. The poles connect to this part of the tent via clips or sleeves. The rain fly then covers all this, forming the second wall. Because the rain fly does not touch the tent body, air circulates between the first and second walls, reducing condensation.

I'm a fan of clip tents (tents that attach to the poles via clips rather than with sleeves that the poles slide into) but there are more tents with sleeved technology to choose from. Whatever you decide on, make sure it sets up easily, has enough room for your intended use, and actually works in a rainstorm. The rain fly on the tent should come almost to the ground and fit snugly. A loose fly will flap in the wind and sag in the rain. The ability to adjust the snugness of the rain fly is bonus because nylon stretches when wet. Finally, get a tent with good zippers or you might as well save money and get a tarp.

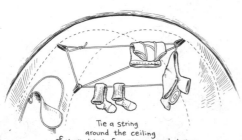

Tie a string around the ceiling of your tent for storage and drying things like stinky socks

Repair Kits

If you don't bring something to fix it, then sure enough, it will break. For this reason alone it's worth having some type of repair kit. Being the weight-conscious guy I am, though, I try to get by with as little as possible. There's nothing worse than that big, heavy repair kit that always gets left behind. The most useful items I've found have multiple uses: cloth tape works well for making bandages and taping broken pieces of gear together again; dental floss works just as well for sewing as it does in preventing gingivitis. A great resource for repair-minded individuals is Annie Getchell's Essential Outdoor Gear Manual. Keep in mind that a repair kit should vary with the kind of equipment you have, the type of trip you are doing, and the length and remoteness of that journey. Sometimes you need a beefy repair kit and other times just tape will do.

Care of Equipment

While nothing lasts forever, with proper care some stuff will come mighty close. Heck, if it wasn't for airport thieves, I would still have some of the original equipment I purchased way back in high school. There are at least three reasons to take care of your equipment. One, it costs money to replace stuff, and while not everyone is as thrifty as me, nobody likes to spend money frivolously (I think?).

Two, when you are out in the backcountry, whatever you have with you is all you have with you. No bopping down to Jed's Outdoor and More to pick up that spoon that seems to have walked off or that shoulder strap the squirrels ate. You need to care for stuff because once it's gone, it's gone. A busted fuel bottle on a climb of Mount Kilamanjaro I did eons ago resulted not only in a change of plans but in our having to carry firewood up to 16,000 feet. I learned some of my lessons the hard way.

Three, losing gear in the backcountry just because you didn't take care of it or put it away is poor style. There is no excuse for littering the great outdoors with our trash or for that matter our favorite sleeping pad. It's a crying shame to be out in the backwoods, thinking you have left civilization behind, only to stumble across someone else's lost socks (especially when they are the wrong size). Keep track of your stuff and keep it in good repair—that way it works when you need it.

Some repair-kit ideas

Duct tape, needle and thread, awl or speedy stitcher, zipper pulls, extra buckles, cord locks, rip-stop tape, p-cord, barge cement, knife/scissors/pliers, tent pole splint, bailing wire, etc., etc. . . .

Bring extra parts for your stove and pump and know how to take it apart. If your pack has lots of little buckles or other small parts that hold it together, bring extras of those.

If you use an inflatable pad, you gotta carry a little REPAIR KIT!

STINKY GLUE

(pffsss!)

DUCT TAPE works okay (not perfect) to fix a hole.

Leave this OPEN while repairing!

Last But Not Least

It would be insane for us to try to describe every item for any trip, and while some folks may want us to describe what type of toothbrush works best in the woods, we just have to leave some stuff up to you. Look at Appendix C for a list of gear to take on any trip and read on to see what else we come up with. Remember, the more you throw in your pack the heavier it gets. Each person has their own favorite item that is essential on any trip, and Mike and I are no different, so figure out what works for you and pack accordingly.

You'll still need a 2nd water bottle or a cup to fill those modern hydration systems

DAY ONE OF A MISERABLE
TWO-WEEK TRIP

TRAVEL TECHNIQUES

When I was a kid about 3 feet tall, my idea of hiking didn't include much walking. My brother and I would run pell-mell down (or up) the trails until we got where we wanted or we tuckered out, in which case we would sit down to rest before taking off again. My parents had the foresight to always take us on trails that had specific destinations—otherwise who knows where we would be now? As I got older this paradigm of blasting from place to place remained with me. I would focus on a destination and then try to get there as fast as possible. Problem was, I would get someplace dead tired, unable to even muster the energy to pitch the tent. My pace would drop from a blistering 5 miles an hour to less than a mile an hour by the end of the day. My feet at the end of a trip would be more blisters than skin. Luckily my knees, feet, and back survived (somewhat) all those early years of life and I have since learned how to conserve energy and avoid damage to my body. The purpose of this chapter is to share some of the wisdom others have taught me over the years to become a more efficient, healthier, and effective backcountry traveler.

Feet

Your feet are your most important resource (next to your brain) out there in the woods, so it makes sense to care for them. Before any hiking trip you should examine them to see how they look, thereby giving yourself something to refer back to when you examine your feet at the end of each hiking day. Trim your toenails at the same time. I have gotten some painful sores on my toes from long toenails. You want to trim them straight across (don't round the corners off) to avoid ingrown toenails.

CLIP!

CUT
TOE NAILS
STRAIGHT!

At the end of each hiking day, when switching from boots to camp shoes, take a minute or two to look over your feet. Dry them out. Get the toe-cheese out from between the toes. Give them a little massage (remember they're your best friends) and look for any blisters or sore spots. I like to check my capillary refill as well. Pinch your toes' nailbeds and watch how long it takes for the blood to return to the white spot your pinching created. In general this should happen within two seconds. Longer times indicate poor circulation, and if your feet have been cold or wet all day you should make sure they stay warm and dry for the rest of the day and throughout the night. Immersion Foot (also known as "Trench Foot") is the end result of feet that have been wet and/or cold for long periods of time. The capillaries begin to leak, and damage to the nerves occurs due to lack of good circulation. Since it can be debilitating both in the short and long term you need to be active in getting those feet warm and dry after a cold/wet day's hike.

On a hot day, soaking feet in a mountain stream after a hard day's hike feels great and cleans them up nicely. Be careful about walking around barefoot however. Even a small cut to the foot can take a long time to heal and be a potential problem in the making, due to the risk of infection. Taking care of your feet is a necessary priority.

When putting on boots, make sure there are no wrinkles or folds in your socks. These can be points of friction that lead to blisters. Clean socks are also important to healthy feet. Dirt, sand, pine needles, etc., create rough spots that act like sandpaper inside a boot. While it's impractical to bring a fresh pair of socks for each hiking day on a long trip, you can keep socks relatively dirt free by wearing gaiters and keeping them out of the dirt. On long extended trips, I rinse out my grungy socks and rotate in a clean pair while those dry.

Lace boots snugly but don't crank them down. I once knew a fellow who laced his boots so tight he would get blisters on his feet—from the tight boots—and on his hands from pulling the laces so hard. The way you walk is far more important than the snugness of your boot (see "Hiking Techniques" just ahead). In fact, hiking with unlaced boots is more likely to result in a lost boot or sprained ankle than a blister. There just isn't enough localized friction. You lace your boots to give your ankles support. Only on steep downhills is it a good idea to really tighten down boots. This helps prevent your toes from sliding into the front of the boot. It's important to loosen boots on steep uphills to allow for more heel lift if you find yourself getting a hot spot.

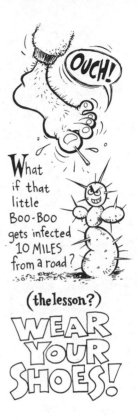

What if that little Boo-Boo gets infected 10 MILES from a road?

(the lesson?)

WEAR YOUR SHOES!

Hot spots and blisters

It's unbelievably important to understand how to take care of blisters. Blisters form from the friction of the foot rubbing against the sides of the boot, due to pressure—and that's why you want to have well-fitting boots. Since friction causes heat, the first thing you feel is a "hot spot." This is the time to stop and take care of the problem, before it becomes a blister. It is well worth the time to stop and fix a hot spot, because if you don't, it will soon be a blister that you will have to stop and fix anyway. Either that or choose to hike in pain.

Sometimes all that's needed to fix a hot spot is to smooth out a wrinkle in the socks. Other times it may be boots that are laced too tight. At the most a piece of moleskin or tape will do. If the hot spot persists or you discover you have a blister, things get a little more complicated. First, if it's a blister you'll want to clean the area with some soap, water, and antiseptic.

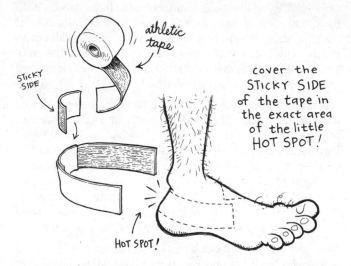

athletic tape

STICKY SIDE

cover the STICKY SIDE of the tape in the exact area of the little HOT SPOT!

HOT SPOT!

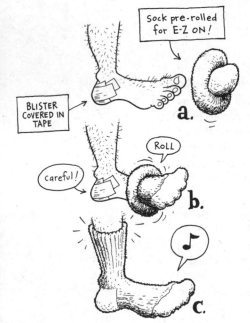

Sock pre-rolled for E-Z ON!

BLISTER COVERED IN TAPE

a.

Roll

careful!

b.

♪

c.

Then, using a knife blade or similar sharp object that has been sterilized (the flame from a lighter works, as does antiseptic), make a small incision at the base of the blister and drain it. This will keep it from popping under uncontrolled circumstances in your boot, which is bound to happen unless it is a very tiny blister. Leave the skin over the top of the blister intact. If you waited so long the skin over the blister has popped or rubbed away, you'll want to treat it like a soft tissue injury and clean it with soap and water.

Your next goal is to find a way to relieve the pressure or friction that caused the hot spot in the first place. There are many different ways to go about this and they work differently for different people, so experiment to see what works best for you. My favorite method is to take moleskin and rub Bacitracin (or some antiseptic gel-type stuff) on the fuzzy side of it and on the blister/hot spot itself. Really goop it on, as the goal is to create a lubricated surface to lessen the friction. Then place the fuzzy side of the moleskin down over the blister and tape it in place. Make sure there are no wrinkles in the tape, or you may be creating a new spot for blisters.

The most popular way to cover a blister is with a doughnut made out of Molefoam or Ensolite pad. This method requires you to cut out a hole in the Molefoam slightly bigger than the blister. The object is to take pressure off the blister by elevating the area around it. Place the doughnut over the blister and fill the inside with Bacitracin or Second Skin, then tape it all down. Now you are ready to go. To get socks on over all this stuff, it's usually better to roll the socks up and then on, versus pulling them on.

If the boot is still causing problems in that same spot, try inspecting the boot to see if there is a fold or something in the material creating pressure. If so, try massaging the fold out or jumping up and down on the boot (remove your foot first) to see if you can soften up the area. People with bony protuberances or spurs on their feet often have trouble as well, due to these spots sticking out. If this is a problem, you should put a doughnut over these areas prophylactically.

Other places I have seen problems with the feet involve the arches. This is a hard place to keep taped up. People with flat feet seem to have the biggest problem here. I recommend taking the insole out of the boot to see if that helps. If you have high arches you might try adding an almond-shaped bit of Ensolite to your foot bed to raise the arch. Other things include keeping the foot clean and dry since problems often start as a salt rash.

You will want to change your blister stuff once in a while. This lets you dry your foot out in these areas and clean them up so you don't develop an infection. While it is best to change bandages once a day you may not have enough blister-care stuff to do this. If it feels good and hasn't been rubbed out of place, I usually leave my blister dressing in place for a couple

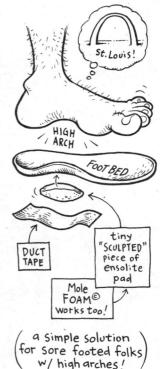

HIGH ARCH

St. Louis!

FOOT BED

DUCT TAPE

tiny "SCULPTED" piece of ensolite pad

Mole FOAM© works too!

(a simple solution for sore footed folks w/ high arches!)

THE DOUGHNUT PAD
technique

MR. BLISTER

cover it all with ATHLETIC TAPE

Pad of a Band-Aid to cover the hole

MOLE-FOAM Doughnut

Tincture of Benzoin (STICKY!)

of days. I change dressings on a rest day when I am not going to be wearing my boots. If it hurts, though, you will want to change it to see what is going on and fix the problem.

TRY NOT TO JUMP with the monster load!

ZOINKS!

CLOMP!

Hiking Techniques

My feet used to blister every time I went hiking. I couldn't figure out what caused it. I'd go tearing down the trail and soon enough, there it was—that familiar hot spot on the heels. It wasn't till I learned to walk flat-footed that I finally solved the problem. When backpacking with stiff boots, you need to make some adjustments to the everyday heel-to-toe stride that most folks use to cruise the city streets. You should strive to place your entire foot flat on the ground and lift it up the same way, rather than touching down with the heel first and rolling the foot onto the toes before picking it up. A flat-footed technique minimizes foot motion within the boot and thus reduces the friction that causes blisters. Deliberately think about where and how you are placing your foot. Not only will this help prevent blisters, but it will also reduce the chance you will roll your foot and sprain an ankle. Walking flat-footed also causes you to shorten your stride and slows the pace down, a small price to pay for healthy feet.

PANTS TUCKED IN!

HIKING IN MUD!

SPLORP!

As far as pace goes, travel at a comfortable rate you can maintain all day. Sprinting out of the block does you no good if three hours down the trail you are having to stop every 100 yards to rest. An ideal pace is one you can keep up mile after mile. Another way to think of it is in terms of time. Shoot for a pace you can keep up, with only a five- to ten-minute rest break every hour. Hiking for an hour at a time assures that you get warmed up and develop a hiking rhythm. A short rest break lets you eat and drink some, but doesn't let your muscles cool down to the point where they stiffen up and make it difficult to get going again. With time and experience you can adapt a style that works well for you. While I no longer sprint for my destination at a grueling 5 miles an hour, I do like to hike steadily with few breaks or none at all. You should be able to chat with your trail mates without huffing and puffing.

Part of maintaining an efficient pace has to do with your conservation of energy. Get in the habit of stepping over rocks and trees (or around them) rather than stepping up on them and then having to step back down. Not only is this easier on the knees, but it saves energy as well.

Monitor your breathing: if you are having trouble catching your breath, then you are going too fast. Slow down and go at a pace that lets you maintain an easy breathing rate without having to stop. When the going gets hard, I'll often set a pace of one step, one breath, one step, one breath. . . . If the going is really hard, it could even be more breaths per step. Slow and steady is far better than short bursts of speed followed by labored breathing as your muscles try to recover from oxygen debt.

If you are hiking with others, set a pace all of you can stick with. This assures you stay together and one person won't get left behind in the dust to fend for themselves. Also keep in mind that reaching your destination is just part of the battle. You still need energy to set up camp and deal with any unexpected problems that come up. Always keep some energy in reserve, instead of spending it all on the trail.

Simply step over obstacles (easy)

Whoa!

Be mindful of your KNEES!

Stepping up! then... Stepping down! (not-easy!)

For steep uphill climbs, the rest-step is a good technique. The idea here is to straighten the leg you just stepped with so your body weight now rests on the bones of that leg. Take a breath or two and then step up with the next leg, straightening it out and giving the muscles a little break. Make your steps slow, smooth, and steady. Rhythm is part of the key to moving efficiently.

While I personally am not a fan of hiking sticks (trekking poles), they are very popular and are useful for taking the strain off knees, especially on downhills. They can also help with balance in some tricky spots. I would just caution you to not become too dependent on them. As a tool, they should add to your balance, not provide you with balance.

Travel Techniques

Rest Breaks

As stated earlier you want to keep most rest breaks short. Five to ten minutes is just enough time to rest some muscles (take your pack off), drink some water, chow on some snacks, and look at the view. Eating and drinking at each rest stop keeps you hydrated and fueled up. This is important because you are expending a lot of calories.

Another type of break you may take on the trail is what I call a "map break." This is just a short little break to look at the map and reconfirm where you are with your hiking partners. Since these breaks are only a minute or two in length, I leave my pack on for them. If there is a rock nearby I might just rest my pack on it. Standing around for long periods of time with a pack on is just a waste of energy, so if your map break starts to drag on, drop the pack.

How much water should you drink?

A general rule of thumb is about 3 to 4 quarts a day. But this really depends on where you are and what you're doing. In a hot desert you'd probably want to double this, but a rest day at camp would require less. A good way to monitor your hydration level is to look at your urine output. Clear and copious is what you are looking for. Dark yellow urine is a sure sign of dehydration (be aware that some vitamins will turn urine a bright yellow). If you are feeling thirsty, then you are already down a liter of water and may have lost 22 percent of your endurance. A headache is also a sign of dehydration. Time to drink up. It's better to drink small amounts of water over time, than to guzzle down a quart in one sitting. This gives your body time to absorb the water, which is why it's so important to be continually drinking all day.

Drink **LOTS** of water!

On a long hiking day, I like to stop for a lunch break. This is typically a longer break (twenty to sixty minutes) to really refuel, rest, and enjoy the place where I am. If I can plan this break in a place with a great view, all the better. It might take me a little while to get warmed up again on the trail, but for me, it's worth it to take a time-out from my hiking day. There are no hard and fast rules for taking breaks; you just need to figure out what works for you. Keep in mind that rest breaks add up, and too many of them will delay your arrival at camp.

Packs

Putting on that behemoth of a pack can be a workout in itself (that's another reason for keeping it light). Here are a few tricks you can use to make it a little easier on your back. The easiest of these is to get a friend to help you out (don't be timid to ask for a hand if that's what you want). But since it feels good to be self-sufficient, here are a couple of ways to do it yourself.

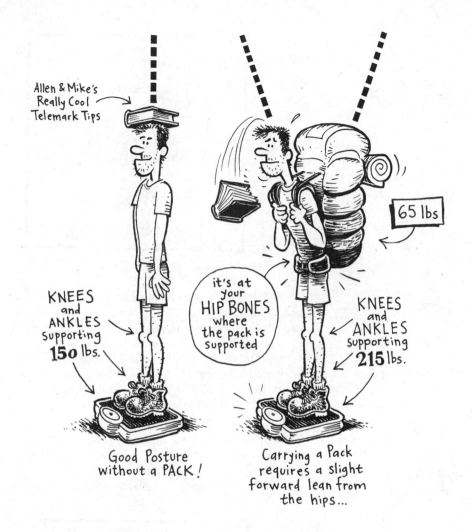

Allen & Mike's Really Cool Telemark Tips

KNEES and ANKLES supporting **150** lbs.

Good Posture without a PACK!

it's at your HIP BONES where the pack is supported

65 lbs

KNEES and ANKLES supporting **215** lbs.

Carrying a Pack requires a slight forward lean from the hips...

Keeping your back straight, lift the pack up by the haul loop or the shoulder straps (for a frame pack, use the frame) onto your knee. Slip an arm and shoulder through the pack strap and swing the pack around onto your back, working your other arm into it. Another method to get the pack up onto your knee is to start by upending the pack so that the bottom of the pack rests on your knee while the top rests on the ground. Then, bending over from the waist, grab the haul loop, and leaning back with your back straight, pull the pack upright onto your bent knee. From here proceed as before. Lastly, you can put the pack up on a rock or a log at about the height of your hips and just slip right into the shoulder straps. This is also a good method for taking off a pack or just taking a short rest break with the pack on.

a. Crossed arms — left hand on the left SHOULDER STRAP — Right hand on HAUL LOOP — Loosen shoulder straps — Loosen Load stabilizing straps

b. Ooooh! — hand on HAUL LOOP — move onto knee — Lift with your Legs! — BOING!

c. hand on HAUL LOOP — Move onto your BACK — lean over forward — left arm thru shoulder strap!

d. Stay leaning forward... — ① Get your other arm thru the shoulder strap — ② CLIP the hip BELT

e. Oooh — ① make a little hop upward. — ② CRANK the hipbelt tight! — SCRUNCH! — ③ Snug down the shoulder straps. — ④ clip the sternum strap. — ⑤ fiddle 'til perfect!

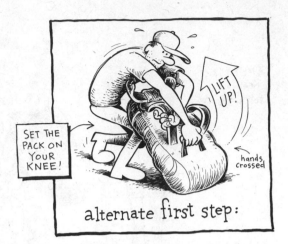

SET THE PACK ON YOUR KNEE! — LIFT UP! — hands crossed

alternate first step:

To take the pack off, you can just reverse any of the preceding ways of putting it on. Some folks like to drop their packs to the ground, but this isn't really good care of equipment. It hardly takes any effort to take out one arm from the shoulder straps, swing the pack around to your knee, take out the other arm, and lower the pack to the ground. Your pack, and the goods in it, will last longer this way.

Once you have that pack on, you will want to make some adjustments. First tighten up the hip belt. The goal is to get the pack to rest on your hips and not on your shoulders. You want the waist belt to sit on top of your hip bones (those are the bones you can feel when

HRRMPH — uppsy daizy!

Don't be afraid to ASK FOR HELP with your pack!

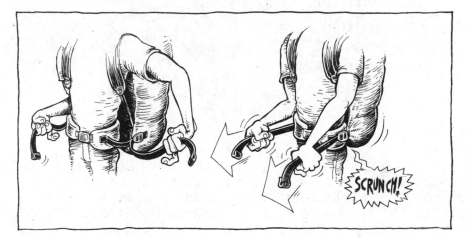

NOODGE

SCOOTCH

TINKER

FIDDLE

TWEAK

You'll probably **FINE TUNE** the pack fit throughout your hiking

the **STERNUM STRAP** is only there to keep your shoulder straps from migrating off your torso

you rest your hands on your sides—the iliac crest). Then crank it down. When most people first get started backpacking they don't tighten the hip belt enough. Don't be afraid to really crank it—you can always loosen it if your legs start to feel numb. Next, snug down the shoulder straps. Packs these days have a plethora of straps to adjust. In general you want to snug them all down. I usually play with my straps all day, adjusting them this way and that, looking for the perfect fit or just changing the way the pack rides for a bit, to give different muscles a break. A comfortable pack may leave you with a few muscle aches at the end of a long day but shouldn't leave you in pain. If you are in pain, you probably need to make some adjustments to the way the pack fits your body. Finding someone who is familiar with fitting the pack is probably the best way to go.

Thermo-Regulation

Temperature control while hiking can be easy as pie or extremely variable—one moment you're hot and sweaty, the next cold and wet. There is probably no way to stay at just the right temperature all the time, but with experience you can become more efficient at wearing the right clothing for the conditions. Your goal should be to stay at a comfortable temperature. Hopefully you can achieve this by adjusting the amount of layers you are wearing.

Soak your hat in water during hot hiking days!

Warm, sunny conditions are the easiest to deal with. T-shirts and shorts will be just as comfortable in camp or at a rest break as they will be hiking. Cool the air temperature down, however, or add some inclement weather, and it starts getting tricky.

Starting off a hike on a cool morning with the clothes you were comfortable wearing in camp is guaranteed to have you overheating ten minutes down the trail. It is better to stash those camp layers in your pack and start off a little chilly, knowing you will soon warm up with the exercise of hiking. In the same vein, when stopping to take a rest break on a cold day, put on a layer right away, so you trap the heat you generated hiking. If you wait until you are cold, you'll have to regenerate the heat you lost, which is wasted energy. Anticipation is half the battle.

Hiking in the rain presents the biggest challenge. You have to choose between getting wet from either the rain or from the condensation formed under the rain gear. As someone who sweats easily, I try to avoid wearing my rain gear whenever I can. In a light drizzle I usually opt to hike with my light nylon wind clothes as protection, since I have found they will shed just enough water to keep me reasonably dry. The same is true if it is raining intermittently. I generate enough heat hiking that I dry out between precipitation events. Only when it is raining steadily enough that I start to get consistently wet do I decide to put on my rain gear. Better to get a little wet via perspiration than soaked by rain. People who don't sweat much can get away with wearing rain gear in most conditions.

A good rule of thumb to remember is that it is better to be warm and wet than to be wet and cold. So if it's raining out and you find yourself sliding down the temperature scale—put on a raincoat. And if you need more layers besides that—put them on too!

Etiquette on the Trail

On the trail, you need to be aware of others. Instead of taking your break in the middle of the trail, move well off to the side, so others can pass by easily. If I am taking a substantial break to eat lunch, fix a blister, etc., I will try to move out of sight as well. Then others can pass me by without even knowing I'm

there. We both keep our sense of solitude, which is important to the wilderness experience.

If you encounter horses or other stock on the trail, move off to the side so they may pass. Horse packers prefer it when you move off to the downhill side of a trail. This way if their horses spook, they go uphill rather than plunging rapidly downhill where it is harder to stay in control. It also helps packers if you greet them as they are riding up on you. The horses are better able to recognize you as a human.

If hiking on-trail, stick to the trail. Stepping off the trail to avoid a muddy patch or a puddle only widens the trail or creates a parallel trail. Eventually this parallel trail will become muddy as well. I have seen places where there are as many as ten parallel trails from hikers trying to keep their boots clean. Boots are meant to get dirty.

Desert areas with highly fragile microbiotic or cryptobiotic soils require you to pay special attention to your hiking route. Since these soils take a very long time to develop and are easily damaged, you should hike on-trail as much as possible. Where this isn't possible hike in dry washes or on slickrock. If you must cross a small area walk on tiptoes and stay in one another's footprints.

When hiking off-trail in delicate areas, such as alpine meadows and arctic tundra, enjoy the view around you instead of

watching your partner's butt. Spread out. Not only will it be more scenic, but by not following in his or her footsteps you lessen the likelihood of creating an unnecessary trail. While plants in these areas are fairly resilient, repeated trampling spells the end for them. Trampled areas take years and even centuries to recover. Wet zones are particularly vulnerable to trampling. If you camp in the vegetative zones, be particularly careful about spreading out and consider moving campsites around each day.

Wildlife

I'm not talking about the rowdy campers across the lake from you. Rather, all the animals who live full-time in the natural world. Be sensitive to these creatures; life is not always easy for them. In addition, we don't appreciate it when they do become conditioned to us. Squirrels who demand that we feed them got that way because careless campers before us left food lying around. Worse yet they may have purposely fed the darned creatures. Hopefully they didn't feed the bears as well.

Enjoy your encounters with wildlife but don't make them change their actions because you need that special picture. Animals big and small are just trying to survive in their natural surroundings. Good style demands that we give them the space they need to do this.

Maps

If you want the ability to travel anywhere in the backcountry, a good understanding of maps is essential. There is only one way to get good at map reading, and that is to study the terrain you see and compare it to your maps constantly. Examine what the map says about the terrain you are about to encounter. Visualize it beforehand, so you know what to expect. Then while traveling compare the map to what you are actually seeing. Refine what your eyes see on the map by comparing it with reality.

The most useful maps for backcountry travelers are the USGS (United States Geological Survey) topographic maps or quadrangles. While there are a variety of scales offered by the USGS, the 7.5-minute topo maps (or 1:24,000) provide the most detail. (See the Trip Planning chapter for information on where to get maps.) Topo maps represent a three-dimensional world in two dimensions. Horizontal distance is represented by the map itself with a scale at the bottom for converting inches on the map to miles on the earth. The third dimension, in the vertical plane, is represented by contour lines (those little brown ones) on the map.

Earthly divisions

As humans, we love to draw lines and divide things up. When it comes to the earth we have split it up into *longitude* and *latitude*. Longitudinal lines are the ones that run north to south and give degrees west and east of Greenwich, England. They start at zero and go up in each direction, west and east of Greenwich, to 180 degrees (at the very eastern end of Russia). Latitude lines encircle the earth east to west and give degrees north and south starting from zero on the equator and going to 90 degrees at each pole. Degrees are further broken down into minutes (60') and seconds (60"). A 7.5-minute map represents 7 minutes and 30 seconds of latitude. In the lower latitudes it also represents 7.5 minutes of longitude, but farther north (say

Scale

Maps come in different scales. A 1:24,000 scale means that each inch on the map represents 24,000 inches on the earth. A 1:250,000 scale would be 1 inch for each 250,000 inches. That's a lot of inches. The bigger the scale, the less detailed the map.

Maps also have a scale that shows what distance on the map represents a mile. You can use this to figure out how many miles you are planning to hike. Take a piece of string and lay it along the route you are planning to take. Mark the starting and ending points on the string and then pick it up and measure the distance between the two points on the scale.

the North Star (POLARIS)

GEOGRAPHIC NORTH POLE

MAGNETIC NORTH POLE (trademark of Canada)

Naughty? Nice? Ooo

Lines of LONGITUDE converge at the POLES

MAGNETIC DECLINATION (this doesn't match the Geographic Pole)

Lines of LATITUDE are PARALLEL

COMPLEX COMPASS

- SIGHTING NOTCH
- SIGHTING TARGET LINE
- SIGHTING MIRROR
- DECLINATION SETTING
- ADJUSTABLE DIRECTION OF TRAVEL ARROW
- NORTH SEEKING NEEDLE
- JEWEL PIVOT POINT
- PARALLEL LINES
- BEZEL RING
- ROTATING COMPASS HOUSING
- BASE PLATE
- LITTLE HOLE
- DIRECTION OF TRAVEL ARROW
- LANYARD

Before using, you'll need to read the compass instructions carefully, maybe twice!

Simple COMPASS

WORKS GREAT!
Do you really need anything more complex?

in northern Alaska), USGS topos increase the number of longitudinal minutes shown east to west. This is due to the fact that longitudinal lines get closer together as they converge at the poles. If the USGS topo maps didn't include more minutes of longitude, these northern maps would get awfully skinny.

Look in the corners of your maps to see the longitude and latitude.

USGS maps contain a lot of data. Not all of it is useful to the backcountry hiker. My goal here is to explain what you need to get started. If you are curious about the rest, the USGS has a nifty little pamphlet that explains it all.

Colors

All the colors on a topo map represent something, and most of them can be used for navigation. Green represents forested areas, but not just any forested area. The tree cover must be dense enough to hide a platoon of troops, or about 40 persons on an acre of land. So an area with a few scattered trees may not appear as green on a map. White signifies all the non-forested areas. This includes meadows, boulder fields, clearcuts, tundra, etc. Blue means water, anything from lakes to intermittent streams that run only part of the year (represented by dashed blue lines). Swampy areas have little blue hash marks to represent the swampy plants. Glaciers and permanent snowfields (it's still water) are dashed blue lines with blue contour lines inside them. Black indicates human-made features such as roads, trails, or buildings. Red also represents human-made landmarks, usually more prominent ones such as highways or such things as survey lines (not visible to the naked eye).

Lastly, purple is used to denote revisions or corrections made from aerial surveys that have not yet been field checked.

Colors can help you determine where you are on a map. If you plan to hike on a trail and it shows you crossing three streams and then going out of the forest and into a meadow, these are all features you can use to locate yourself. Count the streams as you hike by them and take a quick look at the map to see how far apart they are and how far it is to the next one. Check the amount of time it took to go between features. Paying attention to details like this helps you become a better map reader. Simple, isn't it?

It is important to note the date on your map. Look in the lower right-hand corner, just under the name of the map (all USGS maps are given a name, usually related to a significant geographic feature that appears on the map). Some of the maps out there are older than I am. It is worth knowing how old a map is because just like you and me, features change with time. A wooded area 30 years ago may be a clearcut now or vice versa. Same goes with a burned area from a forest fire. Roads and trails may not have been maintained, or new ones may have been built. I have even seen a stream flowing out of a lake change to a different drainage from the one shown on the map. Keep in mind the age of your map.

Orientation

Orienting the map is a good habit. This means lining up the map so the top of the map, which represents north, is literally pointing north. There are a number of ways to go about this. My favorite is to use the terrain, since it forces me to look at the features in the landscape and on the map. Pick a feature, such as a mountain, that you know is correct.

Then rotate the entire map, so things line up from your position on the land. If the mountain is to the east of where you are standing, the eastern edge of the map should be facing the mountain. Double check yourself. If the map shows a stream behind you, there should be one behind you.

You can also use the sun. If it is rising or setting, then the edge of the map facing the sun is the east or the west edge respectively. A compass can easily determine north.

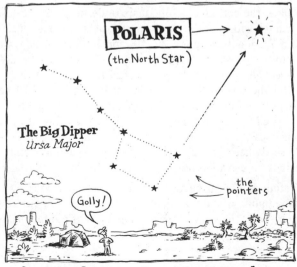

finding North in the nighttime sky

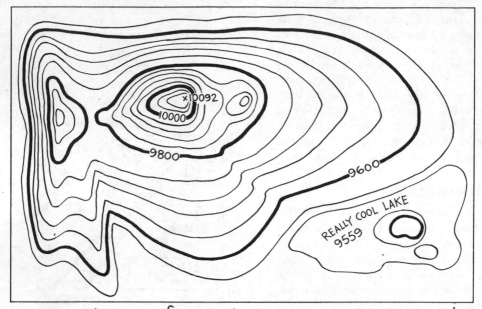

This is the "view" from the little airplane on the next page!

Contours

Perhaps the most useful, yet confusing, things to learn about map reading are contour lines. Spatial intelligence helps, but not all of us are blessed with this. This is where constantly looking at your map and comparing features in the landscape to the ones on the map helps. As mentioned earlier, contour lines let us represent a third dimension (the vertical) on a two-dimensional or flat map. See illustrations.

Look at the bottom of a topo map, underneath the scale, and it will tell you what the contour interval is. Common intervals on a 7.5-minute map are 20, 40, and 80 feet. A map with a contour interval of 40 feet means the distance between each line equals 40 vertical feet. The farther apart the lines, the flatter the terrain. The closer together the lines, the steeper the terrain. Contour lines that are all crammed together indicate a cliff or an overhang. You will notice some of the contour lines are darker than others—every fifth one to be exact. These darker lines are called index contour lines and they include an elevation number somewhere along their length.

Contour lines can be used to tell you when your route is going uphill, when it is going down, or when you are traversing a slope. They also mark features such as mountains, hills, drainages, ridges, etc., all of which can be used to help you

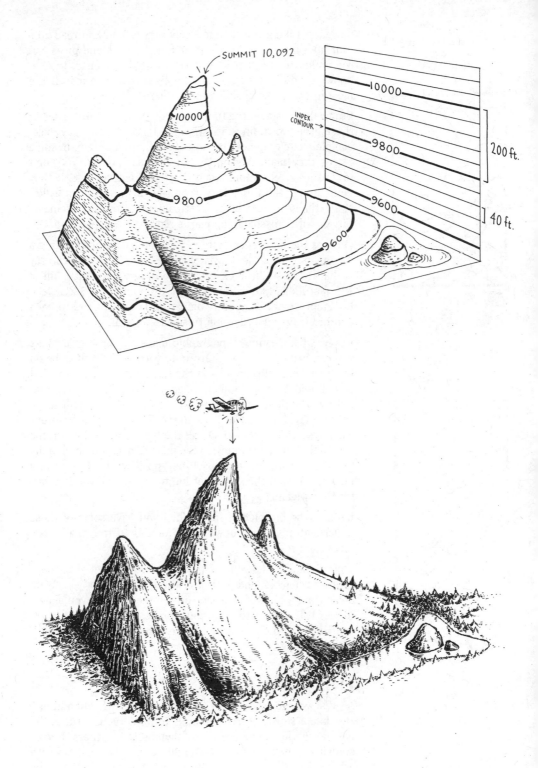

SUMMIT 10,092

10000

9800

9600

INDEX
CONTOUR →

10000

9800

9600

200 ft.

40 ft.

a drainage
or
Stream

Vshaped

DOWNHILL

a ridge

DOWNHILL

Ushaped

navigate. Taking the time to really understand and read contour lines allows you to pinpoint your location and gives you the ability to travel places off-trail with confidence. In fact, knowing how to read the contour lines of a topo map is the most important map skill you can learn.

Study a map; spend the time to look at it and figure out what those little brown lines are showing. Places where they make complete circles denote the top of a hill or mountain. In some places they make V's or U's on the map. If the V's point toward lower elevations, then they represent a ridge. If they point up in elevation, they represent a drainage or valley. Many times there will be a stream marked in a drainage. Circles with crosshatching marks represent a depression.

Perhaps the hardest thing to get a handle on when reading a topo map is the scale of what you are looking at. All I can say is that it takes a little experience to figure out what a hill of 120 feet looks like as opposed to a mountain of 1,200 feet. Looking at your map and comparing known points to each another is how you develop this sense of scale.

Lastly, when reading topographic maps the biggest mistake you can make is to fit the terrain to where you want to be on the map. Make sure to look at the terrain first, establish what you should be seeing on the map, and then see where that puts you. Orient the map to the terrain—does it still make sense? Play devil's advocate with yourself and try to disprove where you think you are. Do all the land features line up the way they should according to the map? If not, you are in a different place. If you are absolutely positive the terrain and map match, and the sun is setting to the south, you had better think again.

Look at the big picture first. When you have some of those larger features nailed down, start looking at the smaller features.

Identify landmarks you are positive about, orient your maps off those objects, and then see where that places you. Walk down the trail a half mile—do you see the features you expect to see? It is only by this continual process of looking at maps, confirming and eliminating features, that you really establish where you are.

Handrails

A great way to navigate on or off-trail is to use "handrails." Just like a staircase has handrails to guide you, so does the natural world. Some are more obvious than others, but by studying a map closely you should be able to come up with a handrail. Visualize what the map is telling you about the terrain ahead. What features are going to stand out? If your route lies along a stream, that is a perfect handrail. The same goes with ridges or hillsides. Stairs often have landings, and so should your natural handrail. Landings tell you where you are along the way, such as the second or third floor. If your handrail is a stream and the map shows another stream coming in from the west, when you reach that stream you have hit the landing and fixed your location. This process of picking out handrails and landmarks along your route beforehand makes navigation easier. Look at your map often to check off landings as you pass them. Try to find features more and more subtle to guide you. I typically hike with my map in hand so that I can peek at it every few minutes if need be.

Compasses

Compasses have their use in map reading, but I caution you not to become dependent on them. They should be a tool to help with navigation, not a crutch you depend on. For a compass to be useful, you still need to be a good map reader, and as a good map reader you rarely need a compass.

The first thing to use a compass for is orientating a map. This is useful in thick trees where you can't see a lot of landmarks. In open country you are able to orient your map off topographical features that you can't see in a thick forest. At the bottom of a USGS map there is a diagram that shows true

ORIENT
THE MAP

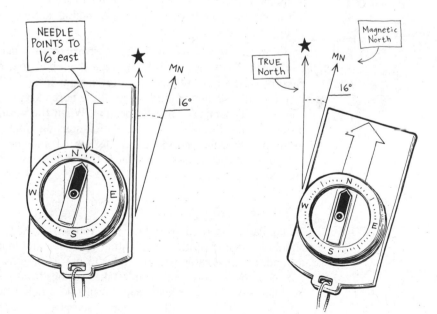

north (a star) and the magnetic declination (MN). Set the compass to read a north bearing and place the edge of the compass along the MN line. Box the needle by rotating the map and compass together and—voilà—your map is now oriented to true north.

Bearings

To take a bearing, orient your map to true north. Then draw a line between your location and where you want to go. Now place the edge of the compass along that line and box the needle by turning the compass housing. The number at the top of the compass is your bearing. To follow this bearing, keep the number set where it is and simply box your needle by turning the entire compass. The compass is now pointed in the direction you want to go. Look down the path indicated by the compass and pick out something as far away as you can see. Now walk to that object and repeat until you reach your destination.

You can also take a bearing from the field. Point the compass at the landmark of interest and box the needle by turning the housing. The number at the top is your bearing. You can walk that bearing if you want as described above, but if you can see where you want to go this seems rather silly. More likely you would use this bearing to locate that object on your map (to help you develop your map skills) or to triangulate. There may be times, however, when it is useful to take a bearing off a landmark because you may not be able to see the landmark during parts of the hike, such as when hiking in dense trees or fog.

To locate the object on your map, first orient your map to true north. Then with the bearing set at the top of your compass, place the edge of your compass at your location. Now turn the entire compass until the needle is boxed keeping the edge of your compass on your location. When the needle is boxed, draw a line along the edge of it starting from your location. You may need to extend this line beyond the compass, but somewhere along this line is the landmark you took your bearing from.

Simple triangulation

Triangulation is used to help locate yourself. Usually you should be able to do this by orienting your map and looking around. In some cases you may want to use a compass. For triangulation to work, you need to take bearings from known landmarks (which takes good map skills). Take a field bearing off a landmark. Then, with the bearing set, place the edge of

BOX THE NEEDLE

The Little ARROW goes in the LITTLE Box

TURN THE ENTIRE COMPASS!

the compass on that landmark, on a true-north oriented map, and box the needle. Draw a line along the edge of the compass. Extend the line as far across the map as you think you need, in both directions if necessary. You are somewhere along this line. Pick another known landmark and repeat the preceding (the farther apart the landmarks the better). Where the two lines intersect is your approximate location. To get even more exact do the same with a third known landmark. The lines will form a triangle (thus triangulation) and your location is somewhere inside this triangle.

Note: As long as you orient your map to true north, you do not need to calculate declination or any other such hoo-hah. Declination is beyond the scope of this book and my brain. There are many good books devoted to map and compass skills. See Appendix B for some of these.

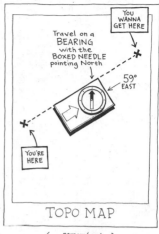

YOU WANNA GET HERE

Travel on a **BEARING** with the **BOXED NEEDLE** pointing North

59° EAST

YOU'RE HERE

TOPO MAP

(remember! orient the map)

GPS

Global positioning systems can be used instead of triangulation to locate yourself. You don't even need to know any landmarks. You do need to know how to find latitude and longitude on your maps however. Of course knowing where you are doesn't do you a whole lot of good if you can't read a map well enough to tell where you want to go. My experience with GPS units is limited to having seen them on the shelves in stores and hearing stories about people lost with their GPS and cell phone calling for help. They knew where they were but didn't know how to get where they wanted to be. While GPS units may be useful for certain things, I am convinced most backpackers can do without them if they just learn good map skills.

GPS

Hello, MR. Ranger, I can't seem to find the trail!

CEL PHONE

TRAIL!

GPS

COMPASS

ALTIMETER

CAMPCRAFT

Once you have figured out how to pack your pack and have made those first couple of miles into the backcountry, the time comes to make camp. Sometimes it's as easy as throwing down your sleeping bag and lighting the stove for some hot ramen and cocoa. Other times it may be more involved, especially if the weather is nasty and it has been a long hard hike. In any case, there are some good principles and techniques to be aware of.

The first of these involves thinking ahead. Look closely at your planned campsite on the map. Will you really be able to get there in the time allotted? If you are unsure, it is good to have a bailout option. Is there going to be water nearby for drinking? Sometimes you have to carry enough water to your campsite for cooking and drinking. Good planning reduces uncertainties and increases the chances for a successful venture. Plan to get into camp with enough energy to deal. There is nothing worse than getting into camp absolutely exhausted, right before nightfall when it's raining. Better to stop at an alternate site while you still have some energy and daylight. While some folks may enjoy leaving greater room for chance, it takes more experience to deal successfully with unexpected circumstances.

Campsite Selection

When looking for a campsite, the first thing to be aware of are the regulations for the area. In many places you are not allowed to camp within 200 feet of water or trails. It varies from place to place, with the highest use areas (national parks, popular wilderness areas, etc.) having the most regulations. These are posted at most trailheads, so look around before you start down the trail.

Next, I try to find a place out of sight. This way I lessen my visual impact on others, and I am less likely to see anyone else. It's okay to pick a spot with a view—after all, who doesn't like to see the sun setting across the mountaintops? But you don't need to pick a place that is in plain view of everyone hiking by. Try camping at the edge of the trees or just off the ridge rather then right on top. I have seen people set up their tents in the middle of the trail. I wonder if they let their kids play in the highway as well.

More important, though, is the actual surface on which you

camp. One of the Leave No Trace principles (see Appendix A) is to travel and camp on durable surfaces. So what does this mean? A durable surface is resistant to impact or, put another way, to our walking around in boots or lounging about the stove. The grass in your yard is durable; the plants in your garden are not. The same is true of different surfaces in the backcountry. Bare ground, as found in impacted campsites, is very durable and makes a good place to camp. Duff (areas where tree leaves have accumulated) is also a very resilient surface, as there are not many plants to kill in these areas. Rocks, sand, gravel, and dry grassy meadows are also resilient areas. Choose camp and kitchen spots that are confined to durable surfaces. Otherwise you create an impacted spot that may or may not recover. If you come across an area that was impacted previously but still has some plant life trying to hold on, choose another spot or you may wipe out those last few remnants of a healthy community.

Once you find a spot with a durable surface for your sleeping quarters and kitchen, take a look around. Are there any dead trees, called "widow makers," that could come crashing down on top of you without warning? How about rockfall? I was once awakened by the sound of a falling rock. Each thud I thought would be its last, but it kept getting closer and closer, stopping 4 feet from my tent. Being that the rock was the size of a refrigerator, I hate to think what would have happened if it had stopped on our tent. Flash floods are another concern, especially in those areas subject to sudden thunderstorms or heavy rains. Be careful of camping in drainages or alongside rivers where this could be a concern. A friend of mine once lost her entire kitchen in Alaska when the river she was camped near, rose 3 feet overnight!

Animals and lightning are two more things to keep in mind. An exposed spot on a ridge, in an open meadow, or next to the tallest tree around may not be the place to camp in a thunderstorm. In the same vein, pitching your tent across an animal trail can lead to some unwanted midnight visitors. Cows have been the villains in most of my experiences.

It's important to spread out your use in a campsite, especially if it's a pristine site and not a well-camped-in spot. By cooking in an area away from your shelter and keeping your packs dispersed, you spread out your impact. Try not to walk the same way between these sites each time. This way you avoid creating trails. Switch into your camp shoes as soon as possible since they are easier on vegetation and soil than lugged sole boots. Your feet will appreciate it as well.

THE WIDOW MAKER

"Look, a nice level spot for my tent!"

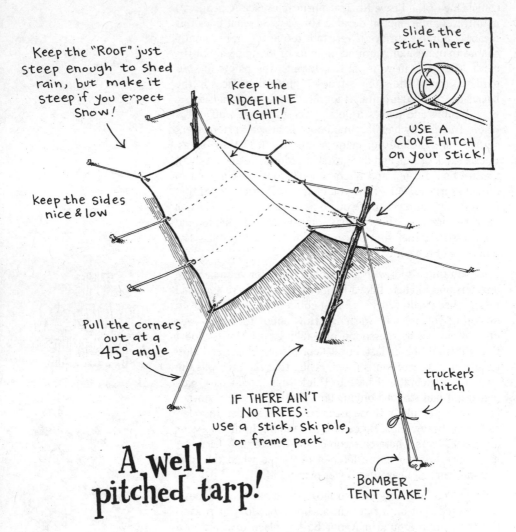

Keep the "ROOF" just steep enough to shed rain, but make it steep if you expect Snow!

Keep the RIDGELINE TIGHT!

slide the stick in here

USE A CLOVE HITCH on your stick!

Keep the sides nice & low

Pull the corners out at a 45° angle

IF THERE AIN'T NO TREES: Use a stick, ski pole, or frame pack

trucker's hitch

BOMBER TENT STAKE!

A well-pitched tarp!

Too thin for sand

Too wimpy for rocky soil

These thin wire tent stakes only work in areas like Alaska tundra, or your lawn.

Tent/Tarp Pitching

Once you have located a durable spot, it's time to set up the sleeping quarters. Avoid depressions and places that collect or funnel water. Ideally you want a smooth spot slightly higher than the area around it so water will flow away from the shelter. It's a big "no-no" to dig trenches around shelters. A smart camper locates a good spot for the shelter rather than impacting a site because they chose poorly. In the same vein, try to avoid moving logs or large stones to make room for your shelter. These objects create important micro-environments for smaller creatures such as insects. How

LAME!

I can't even begin tell you how often I've seen this!

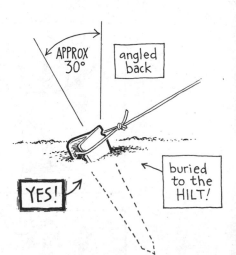

APPROX 30°

angled back

YES!

buried to the HILT!

would you like it if some giant came along and toppled your house? If you have no choice but to move something, at least return it when you're done.

Tents require only that you stake them out. But stake them out well enough so a strong wind won't rip up the stakes when it hits your tent. Staking the rain fly out taut assures it won't sag against the tent body in the rain. A saggy fly is a leaky fly. If the fly is dry when you set up the tent, you may have to tighten it down when it rains since nylon stretches as it gets wet. If you are camped in the woods you can tie the tent's guy lines to some trees.

Tarps, depending on the design, usually require two trees or poles to be pitched. Make the ridge-line tight so it won't sag down when you stake out the corners. In the shelter of trees you can get away with setting the tarp up high for lots of headroom and circulation. This is also the way to go if you are setting up the tarp for shade rather than precipitation. In the wind and rain, however, you want the edges of the tarp set low to the ground. Otherwise the rain just blows in under the tarp. If you need to worry about snow (not so far-fetched in some places or at certain times of the year), make sure the sides are steeply pitched so snow slides off.

hand sized
PERSUADER ROCK
(nice!)

TAP!
TAP!
TAP!

KLONK!

YOUR BOOT...
(ruinous!)

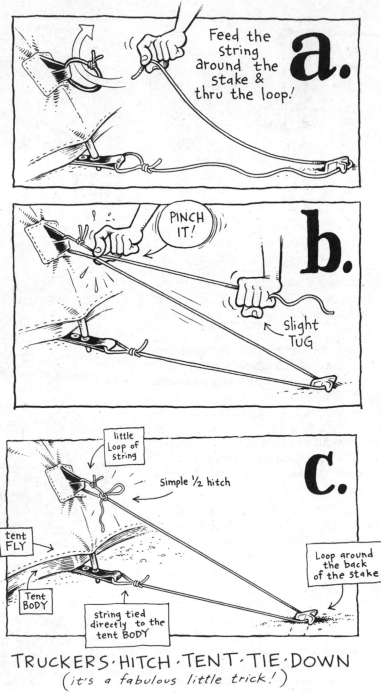

TRUCKERS·HITCH·TENT·TIE·DOWN
(it's a fabulous little trick!)

Otherwise you will be sucking nylon as the weight of the snow pushes the tarp down on top of you.

A Megamid or similar structure can be pitched with a pole or without it. High winds or heavy wet snowfall can cause the pole to snap. Pitching it without the pole creates more room inside. It's worth the weight to carry about 15 feet of parachute cord so you can string a Megamid up between two trees. It also provides a backup should your pole break.

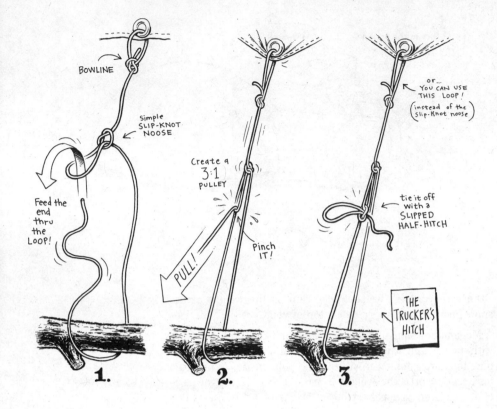

BOWLINE

Simple SLIP-KNOT NOOSE

Feed the end thru the LOOP!

Create a 3:1 PULLEY

PULL!

Pinch IT!

or... YOU CAN USE THIS LOOP! (instead of the slip-knot noose)

tie it off with a SLIPPED HALF-HITCH

THE TRUCKER'S HITCH

1. **2.** **3.**

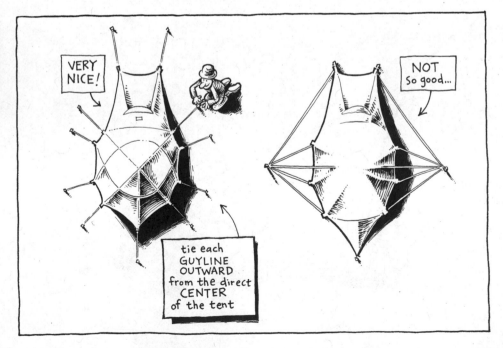

VERY NICE!

NOT So good...

tie each GUYLINE OUTWARD from the direct CENTER of the tent

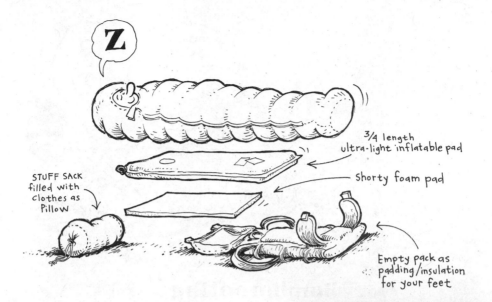

3/4 length ultra-light inflatable pad

Shorty foam pad

STUFF SACK filled with clothes as Pillow

Empty pack as padding/insulation for your feet

There may be times when you choose not to put up any shelter at all, when you would rather sleep out under the stars and are confident it won't rain. Maybe you'll just pitch a tent without the fly because bugs are a problem (otherwise why bother to set it up at all?). You should be comfortable setting up your shelter in the dark if you ever go this route, however, for that one eventuality where you guessed wrong about the weather.

EXPECT a little dew on your bag

Wear a HAT!

TENT

TENT POLES

Have your shelter handy!

ASTRO-BIVY!

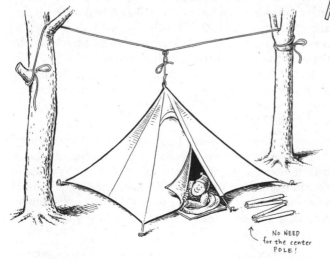

NO NEED for the center POLE!

Bombproofing

This is the practice of making sure all your equipment is properly put away. I can't emphasize enough the importance of this habit. At home (with its four walls and a roof) you can get away with leaving your room a mess, but in the out-of-doors your equipment is sure to get lost or soaked at some point if you don't take care of it.

A bombproof camp is so well organized that if you dropped a bomb on it, you wouldn't lose a single item. All loose items are secured under the tarp, in the tent, or put away in backpacks. No loose wind gear or sleeping pads lying around for the wind to lift away to the next mountain range. Food and eating utensils are stored away in a food bag or some such contraption when not in use. Nothing is left to chance.

ALWAYS KEEP GEAR FROM BLOWING AWAY!

Drying out Mr. Sock

If the wind takes it away, *IT'S GONE* and *IT'S LITTER!*

I always bombproof my camp any time I am away from it or before going to sleep for the night. A sky that starts out clear and sunny may suddenly fill with thunderheads in the afternoon. Those socks left out to dry on a tree limb will be plenty wet by the time you get back from the lake where you were fishing. Boots left out at night can fill with water from a midnight rain or, worse yet, get chewed on by little salt-starved critters like porcupines. Tents need to be staked down well to keep from blowing away.

I leave it to you to learn from experience that weather is unpredictable and gear nonreplaceable (at least till you get back to town). I will always remember the tent I saw floating down a river in the remote Brooks Range of Alaska. I wonder what those people would have done if I hadn't swum out and rescued it. Probably been eaten to death by mosquitoes!

Campcraft

Breaking Camp

When you break camp take the time to really look around and make sure nothing is being left behind. It helps to actually pack up and then move the backpacks away from camp before you do this final sweep. This way there is nothing to distract your eye from the small piece of dental floss that fell out of someone's pocket. Look on the ground and up in the trees. Look where each person had their pack, in the kitchen, and around the sleeping area. Not only are you looking to clean up any garbage, but you are also making sure no one's socks or cameras are still hanging around.

This is the time to replace any sticks or rocks you may have moved. You want to return the spot as close as possible to the way it was before you camped there. Examining your camp will also help you figure out what to do better at the next campsite to reduce impact. Did you create trails to and from the kitchen? Is it obvious where the tent was? Is the vegetation noticeably damaged, or will it spring back? It is by asking questions and reflecting back on what we could have done differently that we learn better ways of doing.

When breaking camp...
SHAKE THE DIRT OUT OF YOUR TENT!

} Dirt!

Kitchens

Just like at a party, the kitchen is where you spend the majority of your time, so you should locate it on the most durable site around. Big flat rocks are my favorite. You can spread out, and it's hard to do much impact to a rock. You do need to be careful around the edges of the rock, however, as the soil is usually shallow here and contains many fragile plants. Pick a rock big enough that you can get yourself, your friends, and the entire kitchen on it. In existing campsites stick to areas that have already been laid bare to earth. While you want to spread out from your shelter in a pristine area, in an impacted site it doesn't matter, unless you are bear camping (see Chapter 6).

If the kitchen is in a less-than-ideal spot, consider moving it between each meal to disperse the impact.

Stoves

Pick a spot for the stove where you won't start a forest fire. This is particularly true for a stove that must be primed, as gas will sometimes spill out of the spirit cup. Keep a pot of water close by in case a fire does get started. This can also be the pot ready to go on the stove once it's fired up.

Keep fuel bottles away from the kitchen and never fill the stove in the kitchen area. This helps assure you won't light

FOOF!

Poor Stove Lighting technique!

Stove with RAW FUEL in the Spirit cup

Flick!

proper stove-lighting technique!

your fuel supply on fire. Another classic mistake that gets made time and time again is filling the fuel tank while the stove is running. Don't ask me why, but I have heard more than one story of flaming fuel bottles due to this. If you ever experience this, remember to smother the fire with dirt, not water—water only floats the fuel and sends it to new places. A burning fuel bottle will not explode, so don't throw it like a hand grenade. Instead, try to smother the flame by carefully placing the lid or some other object over the opening. Don't burn yourself!

To light a white gas or liquid fuel stove, you must first preheat, or prime, the stove. This is done by adding pressure to the fuel tank, usually 10 to 15 pumps (you do not want to over-pressurize the tank or the stove will not burn correctly). Then fill the spirit cup with gas. The directions for your stove will explain how best to light it. Once the spirit cup is filled you turn off the gas (filling it about halfway works fine vs. filling to the tippy top and having it spill over). You must now light the fuel in the spirit cup. A lighter or match works for this. I prefer lighters because you can strike the flame while holding the lighter to the spirit cup. This is a bonus in windy conditions when it is difficult to get a lit match to the stove. Carefully hold the flame to the fuel. Do not bend over the stove while doing this. Occasionally the fuel can flare up, especially when it is warm or if you are relighting a stove that has not been off for long. Having your face over the stove is a recipe for disaster.

Once the spirit cup is lit, let the flame die out or almost die out. The stove is now hot, and the fuel will be converted from liquid to vapor as it flows though the generator. If a small flame in the spirit cup still exists, simply turn on the valve and the stove should light. If not, strike your lighter at the top of the stove when you turn on the valve. This should light it. Once again be careful to keep your body and face away

(NICE!) ONE DROP, plenty!

(YIKES!) VALDEZ

GLUG! GLUG!

SPIRIT CUP

ALTERNATE FILLING TECHNIQUES

from the top of the stove. A stove that is not properly primed will flare up. If you hear a sputtering sound, rather than a soft hissing of gas when you open the valve up, the stove is not primed enough. Let it cool down completely and prime again.

If the stove will not light after repeated attempts or the flame does not burn well (i.e., it is yellowish and/or not very strong) the stove may need to be cleaned. Since there are a lot of different stoves, you should refer to your stove's directions for cleaning information. Once the stove is lit you may add more pressure to the fuel tank if you want it to burn hotter.

A butane or cartridge stove may simply be turned on and lit, so there's not much to say about them.

When turning off your stove, blow out the flame after you have closed the gas valve. This keeps the flame from leaving behind carbon deposits that clog the jet. Additionally, when you are all done with your stove and it has cooled down, consider packing it up in a clean stuff sack for the night. This keeps dirt from blowing around and clogging the jet orifice where the gas comes out. This is especially important if the kitchen is in a sandy area.

Fires

There is a definite skill to lighting and cooking on fires. For the most part fires are rarely used anymore for cooking due to the advent of good stoves and the impact fires have on the

Stoves in tents

Most stove and tent manufacturers don't recommend cooking in your tent. This is because of the danger from carbon monoxide buildup and fires (tents are highly inflammable). Carbon monoxide is produced by the burning of a stove and can be deadly if allowed to build up in a small space. It is odorless and causes drowsiness and then death.

If for some reason you feel compelled to cook in your tent, then at least light the stove outside it and keep the tent well vented. Personally I never cook in my tent, although I have cooked outside the door from time to time.

Yikes! that's a BIG fire ring!

81

Tips for fuel efficiency

- Use a wind screen. Wind sucks the heat away from stoves and pots. Cook in a sheltered spot if possible.

- Use a lid on that pot. This keeps the heat in.

- Dark or black pots absorb more heat.

- Use a heat exchanger such as the one made by MSR.

- Don't over-boil water or heat the atmosphere with the stove. Leaving a pot of water on a roaring stove after it boils is a waste of fuel, as is leaving the stove on when you are not ready to start heating water or food.

TRIPLE FOLDED Bandana as "POT GRIP"

DON'T USE a POLYESTER GLOVE!

just make a TINY FIRE!

The POT will get BLACK!

SET THE POT diretly on the hot coals!

ECO-GROOVY L.N.T. MOUND FIRE!

COOKING ON A FIRE!

the 3 rock COOKING FIRE!

The POT will get BLACK!

Easy to feed the flame with small Sticks

BALANCE the POT on 3 ROCKS

a tiny FIRE is fine!

(always) Build an L.N.T. FIRE!

environment. I am not talking about forest fires but the abundance of ugly fire rings, trees with all the lower branches broken off to be used for fuel, and forest floors devoid of any kind of wood for hundreds of feet around popular campsites.

If for some reason you feel compelled to cook over a fire, here are some ideas. One, make it a minimum-impact fire. Two, make sure there is abundant wood around. By this I mean dead and downed wood. Three, a cook fire is a small fire, built in the middle of three rocks which support the pot. You will need to use small pieces of wood for this, but that's okay since they burn hotter. You can use dried cow dung as well—it's what a large part of the world's population uses.

To get the fire started you can use fire starter if you have any. Typically I start a fire using very fine pieces of wood and slowly adding larger pieces. By fine pieces I mean the smallest twigs you can find, about the thickness of pencil lead. You can add twigs the size of pencils to it once it's burning. If there are no small twigs around, then you can whittle some fine shavings from a bigger piece of wood. Make a pile of this fine wood about the size of your fist. Stack some slightly larger pieces (smaller than a pencil) around it in a loose tepee. Strike a match or hold a lighter flame to it and it should go. You can

blow gently on it to help it out if it starts to smolder. The drier the wood, the easier it will light. Look for dry twigs under trees with thick foliage. If you are whittling shavings, the driest wood will be near the center. Dry out other wood by keeping it near the fire.

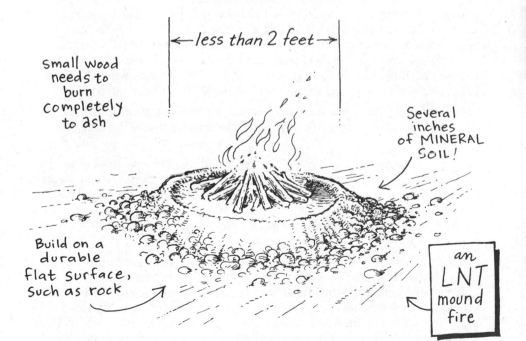

Minimizing the impact of campfires

In popular camping areas it's all too easy to see the impact that fires are having on the landscape: fire rings everywhere and no dead and downed wood (an important source of nutrients for the soil). Heck, you can even see the impact of campfires in remote places. I remember hiking up a ridge in the North Cascades above the Spider Glacier for the view and what did I find? The only tree on this ridge had been chopped up and burned in a fire ring. Sad but true.

To reduce the impact of fires ask yourself a few questions:

- Do local regulations allow for the use of fires?
- Is abundant wood available? At tree line and in heavily impacted sites this is not going to be the case.
- Are there existing heavily used fire rings? If so, use them.
- Is the danger of starting a wildfire high? If so, don't build a campfire.

If you have determined a fire would be acceptable and there are no recent heavily used fire rings around, you should build a minimum-impact fire. The easiest method is to find a place with abundant mineral soil. This is sandy/gravelly soil lacking in nutrients and organic materials. Dry streambeds or riverbanks and shorelines below the high water mark are all good places to build a fire, since they are usually composed of mineral soil. Dig a shallow pit in the soil (about an inch deep) and build the fire in the depression. Don't build a fire ring because they serve no purpose, and the fire scars the rocks with black carbon. When you are done with the fire, scatter the ashes and fill the pit back in.

If for some reason, you can't find a large enough area of mineral soil, don't despair. You can always build a mound fire. To build one of these you take a ground cloth or fire blanket and fold it up so it is about 2 feet by 2 feet. Lay this in the spot chosen for the fire and cover it thickly (6 to 8 inches deep) with mineral soil. You often find mineral soil under the roots of trees that have fallen over or can take it out of a streambed. Build your fire on top of this mound. You won't be able to have a huge blaze, but there really is no need for a Texas A&M fire in the woods anyway.

Make sure your fire is out when you head to bed (you can douse it with water). In the morning scatter the ashes, and return the mineral soil to the spot whence it came.

Remember to always use dead and downed wood for your fire. Leave living trees alone, so they can go on producing oxygen. It's a good idea to use only pieces of wood smaller around than the size of your wrist. This leaves the bigger pieces of wood on the forest floor, where they decay and add nutrients to the soil. It also ensures your fire will mostly burn down to ash and not charcoal, which is harder to disperse.

Ever find yourself in a place littered with fire rings? If so, feel free to do something about it! Decide which fire rings are most likely to get used again and leave those in place. With the others, gather the ashes and disperse them widely. Take any garbage that was in the ash and carry it out with you. Then scatter the rocks from the fire ring. If possible toss them in a stream so the carbon will eventually wash off. Lastly, scatter some detritus from surrounding areas so the old fire ring becomes invisible.

Cooking

Once you get your stove or fire lit it's time to get the pot on and the water going. In the interest of conserving fuel, it's good planning to have your pot filled with water and ready to go before lighting the stove. Once it boils turn the stove off or have food ready to go so you can start working on the meal. Being efficient around the stove lets you get by with carrying less fuel. This keeps your pack lighter.

Safety is also a big concern around a stove or fire. Not only is there the flame of the heat source to worry about, but pots of boiling water can also cause bad burns. Be careful with pots of hot water when picking them up from the stove, stirring them, or pouring hot drinks from them. Sitting close to the stove is a dangerous position to be in should that pot tip over or get knocked off. Getting boiling water down your pants leg and into your boot will put a hurt on you. Should you ever get burned by water (or by grabbing something hot like a fry pan), the first thing to do is soak the burn in lots of cold water as fast as possible. This will help take the heat out of the burn and lessen the damage from it. Then apply first-aid techniques, which can be learned from some of the manuals listed in Appendix B.

Baking

Baking is a wonderful thing to do on camping trips. I love bread products, so almost any trip I do will involve some baking. Pizzas for dinner or cinnamon rolls for breakfast are my favorites, but I never complain about quiche or braided dill cheese bread either. While I won't go into recipes here, I will give you some ideas on how to bake.

The biggest secret to baking in the backcountry is keeping your heat source low. Too much heat and you burn things. So figure out how to turn your stove down. Some stoves have lots of knobs and valves to turn, that effectively let you control the heat. Other ones may simmer better if you just depressurize them a little (this can be done by turning the stove off, blowing out the flame, and then releasing some of the pressure in the fuel tank by unscrewing the lid). You may also elevate the pan above the stove so less heat reaches it. Try this with the wind screen or some rocks. The thicker the pan you use, the better off you will be. Thin pans tend to let the heat concentrate in one place while a thicker pan distributes the heat better, keep this in mind when looking for a fry pan to buy.

Rotation is the next key. Offset the fry pan on the stove so only one part of it is over the flame. Then rotate it every few

the AMAZING
EATING BOWL
AN OWNERS MANUAL and GUIDE
to
The Joys and Dangers
of Backcountry Dining

PARTS of YER BOWL:
the little finger tab
the LID
the inside "gutter"
the BOWL
eat from here...

YOU CAN COOK in your BOWL!
You can put cous-cous, oatmeal or spud pearls in the bowl and Add some boiling water and put the lid on!

insulate the bowl in a pile jacket (make sure the lid has "POPPED") wait **10** minutes, then enjoy!

CLEAN that BOWL!
① EAT EVERYTHING You COOK! Yummmy!
this may sound easy, but you'll need to plan ahead at each meal so you don't have left-overs!

② BOIL SOME WATER! You won't need much, just a splash!

③ POUR THE WATER INTO the BOWL!

④ SNAP ON THE LID and SHAKE SPLISH! SPLISH!
Be careful, that water is HOT and the lid will...

⑤ **POP!**

⑥ SHAKE it some more then Sump (or broadcast) the "GREY" water...

Philosophy of food

Before embarking on a trip you will need to decide on a philosophy regarding food for the trip. Most of the time I like to take lots of good food and feast while I am on a trip. Although in the past I have literally done trips living off the land, I usually got pretty hungry. Sometimes I do trips in between these two extremes, taking simple foods that don't need much cooking or none at all. It just depends on my goals for the trip. If you want to go whole hog, there are a number of excellent books on camp cuisine out there providing ideas for rations and recipes. My favorite is The NOLS Cookery but I'm probably just biased. Look around the bookstore and I am sure you will come up with some good ones. It's worth it to cook good food out there—it makes the whole experience that much better.

Simple Quick Bread

½ cup white flour

½ cup whole wheat flour

¼ cup powdered milk

1½ tsp. baking powder

2 Tbs. of oil, butter, or margarine

2 tsp. brown sugar

¼ tsp. salt

1¼ cups of cold water

Mix all ingredients and pour into a well-greased pan. Cook covered for about 15 minutes or until done. Get creative by adding brown sugar, nuts, and dried fruit. Or try cheese and spices for something really different.

minutes so another part of it is over the flame. This helps distribute the heat around. You can mark the spot you started from with a rock and then keep spinning in the same direction a little bit at a time. If you can, check the bottom of whatever you're baking from time to time. This lets you see what parts need more baking.

The last trick is figuring out how to heat the top of the darned thing. I can think of three methods. One is to use the nifty little backpacking ovens that are on the market now. You simply cover the pan and stove with one of these and rotate from time to time. Mike used one to bake a double layered chocolate cake in a blizzard!

The other method is to build a twiggy fire on top of the fry pan lid. The heat from this will help bake the top, and you can keep heating the top even after the bottom is done. Never light a twiggy fire on top of your pan with white gas; you could ruin your dinner if the gas gets into the food. Instead try lighting the twigs with the flame from the stove and then placing them on the lid.

Finally, you can use my favorite method. This is the flip technique, which works well for certain bread products like pizza or coffee cake. With this method you simply cook one side on a low heat and then flip it over to cook the other side. Flipping takes some skill and practice, but it's a good way to win friends and influence people. Flip it just like a large pancake by creating lift with the fry pan and turning with a spatula. Once you have flipped the pizza dough you can

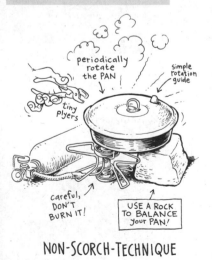

periodically rotate the PAN

simple rotation guide

tiny plyers

careful, DON'T BURN IT!

USE A ROCK TO BALANCE your PAN!

NON-SCORCH-TECHNIQUE

Simple Yeast Bread

1½ cups of whole wheat flour

1½ cups of white flour

½ cup powdered milk

2 Tbs. sugar

1 Tbs. yeast

1 tsp. salt

¼ cup oil, butter, or margarine

1½ cups warm water

The water needs to be warm, but not hot. Test on your wrist; it should feel slightly warm. Mix sugar with the water, and add yeast. Let this mix set for 5 minutes until it gets foamy. Add half the flour and mix for 3 minutes. Add remaining ingredients and mix to get a thick dough. Knead the dough on a flat surface (like your Ensolite sleeping pad, unless you're in bear country) for about 8 minutes. Add more flour if dough gets sticky. Use right away or let rise. Rising creates a fluffier bread but isn't always necessary. Start by creating a round shape with the dough and placing in a warm place. Keep oiled and covered so it doesn't dry out. Keep it warm for about an hour, or until it doubles in size. Bake for 30 to 45 minutes.

TINY STICKS ONLY!

Fire directly on the FRY PAN LID!

BAKING!

the important WIND SCREEN

THE **TWIGGY** FIRE!

add toppings. Or you can flip the pizza with the toppings already on and get the fried cheese effect.

Water Treatment

Unfortunately the days of dipping your cup into the stream and having a drink are over. You can do this if you want, but you run the risk of contracting a water-borne disease like *cryptosporidiosis, campylobacterosis,* or *giardiasis* (the most common). If you are hiking outside of North America, there are even more potential problems with the water—so watch out! Diarrhea and stomach cramps are the usual outcomes in North America of drinking infected water. Depending on the organism, symptoms may not appear for four to ten days after ingesting untreated water. Symptoms may last anywhere from two to eleven days and believe me, these are very unpleasant days. You should find a doctor if you feel you have contracted a water-borne illness.

FLOATIES

SINKIES

Technical terminology defining the delineation of backcountry H₂O bottle particulate content.

Memories of Yester-Year
Sadly, you can no longer drink un-treated water!

Prevention of water-borne illnesses is rather easy and water disinfection is how you achieve it. There are three primary ways to disinfect water: boiling, halogens, and filters.

Boiling

The act of bringing water up to a rolling boil will effectively kill all the pathogens in water. There is no need for it to boil five to ten minutes or to adjust for altitude as is often suggested. The time involved in bringing the water to a boil creates enough thermal action to kill the little buggers. Boiling water is the most effective way to sterilize it. If you plan to make something with water such as pancakes, you do not have to disinfect it beforehand. The simple act of cooking will kill any pathogens that existed in the water. Just don't lick the raw mix out of the bowl, and don't undercook the pancakes.

Halogens

Chemicals like iodine and chlorine can be used to disinfect water. Simply add the right dose to the water and let it sit for the recommended time—in most cases, the water will be safe to drink after this. Since halogens work by bonding to the pathogens, they work best when there is not a lot of other organic material around. If your water is really dirty, you may need to use more of a halogen, or wait longer. You also can't add drink mixes to your water until after the water is ready to drink. The colder the water is, the longer you have to wait as well. One drawback of halogens is they make the water taste funny. Another drawback is that chlorine and iodine are not effective at killing *Cryptosporidium,* so you still run some risk where this protozoan is present. Iodine tablets such as Potable Aqua have long been my favorite way to disinfect water, due to the

IODINE

I 53

Atomic Wt.126.9045

SNIFFF!
very slight chemical odor...

slightly BROWN color

convenience of using them and the fact they don't weigh much. If you disinfect water in your water bottle with halogens, remember to get the threads as well.

Filters

Filtering water is the quickest way to quench your thirst on the trail. Break out the filter, stick one end in the water, the other in your water container, pump, and there you go, drinking water. Filters come in all shapes and sizes, so read up on what they will and won't filter out. "Absolute pore size" determines what a filter can or cannot filter out. Some filters have pore sizes that only work for *giardia* while others will take out virtually everything. Guess which ones are harder to pump. In general, filters with a pore size of 1 micron or less

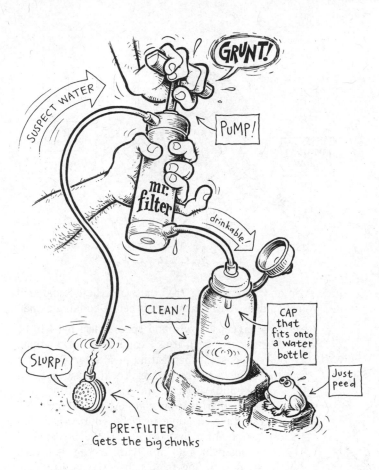

PRE-FILTER
Gets the big chunks

will work fine for most backcountry users. No filter has a small enough pore size to filter out viruses, so if you are hiking in countries where this is a problem, get a filter that has an iodine element.

The biggest disadvantage to filters, besides extra weight, is that they clog. Even in relatively clear water, a filter will clog up with repeated use. So find a filter that is easy to clean. Dirty water should be pre-filtered or left to settle before pumping it through your filter.

Tip: As a backup, carry a halogen in addition to a filter in case the filter breaks, gets clogged, or gets lost.

Sanitation and Cleanliness

If you and your friends want to remain happy campers on your trip, sanitation is important. After taking that walk in the woods (see "Pooping in the Woods") it's important to wash those hands. Take your water bottle and some soap with you and wash up by scrubbing your hands vigorously with a

use your tea bag as a cleansing facial wipe,
...but don't rub too hard!

little soap and water (just a drop or two of liquid soap will do). You should also clean those hands before cooking dinner.

Finger tips work fine for cleaning kitchen stuff...

Pots, pans, cups, bowls, and spoons also need to be cleaned after each use. I can't think of anything more disgusting then eating meal after meal with the same dirty cookware. Yuck! Besides being unpleasant, you run the risk of getting "the mung" (diarrhea) or some other food-borne illness. Take the time to clean your dishes. Dry scrape them first to get out the bigger food scraps (which go in a garbage bag) and then scrub with fingers and hot water. A little soap can help as well. Never wash dishes in a stream unless bear camping or regulations call for it. It's better to wash 200 feet from water sources and then disperse the dirty dishwater by flinging it out over a wide area.

Some folks enjoy a little bathing on their wilderness trips. While it's okay to take a swim in a lake or river to clean off the accumulated sweat and dust of the trail, it's not okay to use soap in these lakes or rivers. Soap, even the biodegradable type, has an adverse effect on aquatic organisms that are very sensitive to their environment. If you feel the need to soap up then take some pots of water 200 feet or more from the water source and lather up sparingly and rinse off there. This keeps the soap out of the water source and reduces your impact on all the other creatures who use that water. A skin brush is also a great way to get clean in the woods. Simply brush yourself all over to shed the outermost layers of dead skin cells and dirt. It really does feel good.

Tips for women

It's important to know what to do during that special time of the month. Now I may not be the expert at this (or even experienced), but I have spent a bunch of time camping with some very experienced women, so let me share what I have learned from them. Physical exercise, a change in environment, and the resulting stress can sometimes lead to changes in a woman's cycle. Cessation or a heavier than normal flow can be the outcome of this. There is nothing to worry about in either case, but since the second case can create some inconveniences, it's a good idea for women who haven't yet spent a bunch of time backpacking to carry one-third more tampons or pads than they might normally use. One friend of mine suggests carrying something even if you're sure you won't be getting your period. "You never know," she says.

As for disposal of tampons and pads, a system of one or two plastic bags inside a small stuff sack works fine. You can throw the used sanitary material in the bags and tie them up. The stuff sack protects the plastic bags from tearing and offers a visual cover. Simply dispose of the plastic bags when you get home. If you are worried about smell, you can crush some aspirin up in the bag. A bandanna, baby wipes, or moist towelettes are also nice to have along.

Note: When in bear country, hang used tampons with the food bags at night or when away from camp.

Pack it in; pack it out

This old Forest Service refrain pretty much says it all. If you can pack it in, you should have no problem carrying it back out. In fact, I often pack out the extra trash I find on the trail. Develop a good system for dealing with trash—then you won't leave any behind by accident. I keep a small plastic bag handy for all those incidental scraps of garbage that manifest themselves throughout the day. Another garbage bag in with the food bag makes collecting food scraps and other garbage associated with cooking a snap.

Pooping in the Woods

The one thing most first-time backcountry users are nervous about is going to the bathroom when the nearest toilet seat and roll of TP is half a day's hike (or more) away. Well, relax a little—it's really not that difficult. You may even find the woods are more enjoyable than a fully decked out watercloset.

Human waste is a major source of pathogens including *giardia, campylobacter, hepatitis,* and on and on. Yuck! For this

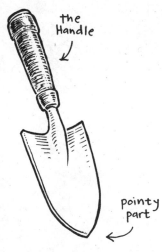

the Handle

pointy part

THE TROWEL

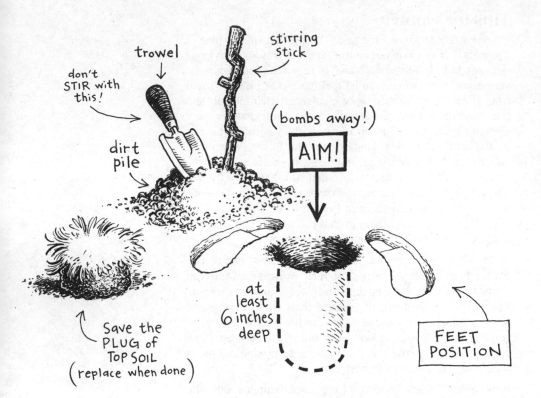

don't
STIR with
this!

trowel

stirring
stick

dirt
pile

(bombs away!)

AIM!

Save the
PLUG of
TOP SOIL
(replace when done)

at
least
6 inches
deep

FEET
POSITION

reason we want to dispose of it in a way that keeps it from spreading throughout the ecosystem and maximizes its decomposition. Burial in the ground is the best solution to this (other than packing it out to some waste-treatment plant).

So the most important thing to remember when taking a poop is how to dispose of it properly. Going behind the nearest bush, dropping the drawers, and letting fly is not acceptable. Not only is it offensive to other campers who may wander by, but it has a negative effect on the environment. Improperly cared for waste can enter the water system directly or via another animal (who may have tried to recycle your waste by munching on it). In addition, insects love to land on excreta and may spread it to your bologna sandwich or somewhere else, and this is unacceptable!

So how do we go about pooping in the woods? Well, the first thing I like to do when the urge hits me is go for a nice walk. By taking a five- or ten-minute jaunt through the woods, I gain some privacy and help spread out the distribution of dumps being taken around the campsite. Next I look for a site that is well away from any water sources (200 feet minimum) or potential water sources, such as dry drainages or low

Pooping Positions:

the CLASSIC SQUAT.

the telemark.

one hand back.

Both hands back with rock assist

one hand back with ROCK assist.

improvised toilet "Seat" using a downed tree or properly positioned rocks.

the HANG (tree assist)

modified hang using a LOG as balance stabilizer.

Natural BUTT WIPES!

These are **all** wonderful alternatives to toilet paper!

spots. If I can find a room with a view, all the better. Nothing like taking a dump in a beautiful spot with lots of privacy (hint: make sure your room isn't in someone else's view).

Look for a spot with enough soil to dig down several inches (6 to 8 being the ideal). What you really want, soil-wise, is nice, dark, rich-looking soil. This is the organic layer of earth as opposed to the mineral soil which lacks organisms to help your poop decompose. Organic soil will be the uppermost layer of soil. If the spot is shaded, then it helps the soil retain a little moisture to aid in decomposition, but it's most important to keep it out of water sources.

Use a small trowel to dig a hole (referred to as a cathole) just big enough to contain your deposit. If the spot you chose has plenty of vegetation, start this hole by cutting a plug out of the ground and then excavating the soil beneath this. You can replace this plug when you're done. If the ground won't hold together enough to make a plug, scrape the very top away before digging so you can use this surface debris to help disguise the spot when done.

After you make your deposit in the hole, toss in some soil and give it a stir with a stick. This will help with the decomposition. Then finish burying it. Replace the plug if you have one or scatter some of the duff you scraped away initially over the top. Make it match the ground cover. I would consider it an honor to find and dig up a well-camouflaged cathole. Well, maybe not, but you should still shoot for a well-disguised cathole. (One of the reasons to spread out from camp when pooping is to keep everybody from digging up each others' catholes.)

Your choice of wiping material is entirely up to you. I personally like to go all natural—smooth sticks and stones are my favorites, although at times I will use moss if it is growing in abundance. Moist snow is also good wiping material because it's both a wipe and a wash. Avoid using living plants if possible—not only is it bad for the plant, but in some cases you may discover you're allergic to the plant. Ouch!

Collecting wiping material on your walk into the woods is easy. Experiment with different sizes, shapes, and textures of objects and you will soon know what works best. Some old-time mountain men carried a "wiping stick" with them, which they would wipe clean after each use. In other countries the left hand is often used for wiping and then well cleaned. I can't recommend either of these last two practices for back-country travelers due to the risk of cross contamination, but it does illustrate other alternatives to paper dependence.

The advantage to natural wiping materials is you don't have to pack them out. Just leave them scattered around the dump site. If you prefer to stick with the toilet paper (TP) line, then come prepared to carry it out! A plastic bag dedicated to carrying used TP works great and is the best alternative to burying it,

a real life
REVOLTING
lack of
backcountry
etiquette

ewww!

Stinky
smell!

USED
Toilet
Paper

flys

UN-BURIED
POOP!

an all too
COMMON SIGHT
along the trail!

which I don't recommend. Burying or leaving the TP behind is not acceptable because it disintegrates very slowly. Just think of the times you have come across some nasty old TP at a car-camping site.

Burning TP is another option that is often touted. In reality, though, it is difficult to burn TP due to its moisture content after wiping. Also—heaven forbid—forest fires have been started by people attempting to burn their TP. Burning TP is not recommended.

If you are nervous about using nature's TP, then start out using natural materials and use your TP for that final wipe. Then you won't have as much to carry out. Keep in mind that a large part of the world's population doesn't even use TP.

The above guidelines apply to most situations that backpackers in the United States are likely to encounter. However, please see the "Special Considerations for Special Environments" section at the end of this chapter for further information on pooping outdoors.

Washing up

Washing those hands after you defecate is an important part of the entire process. Get someone to pour some water over your hands and scrub them really well. The action of scrubbing is just as important, if not more so, than the use of soap in killing off bacteria. The mechanical action helps to break down germs and remove them from the skin. That's why surgeons scrub, and you should too. Please be aware that washing your hands directly in the stream or close beside it defeats the purpose of keeping pathogens from our bowels out of the water system in the first place. Please wash hands away from shore.

Urinating

When taking a leak, try to keep it off delicate vegetation, as mineral-starved animals will often tear up

Listen up LADIES!

when tied to the outside of your pack **SUNLIGHT** will dry and sterilize (well, sorta) your glorious PEE RAG!

YUMMY, URINE SOAKED DIRT!

these plants as they try to get their salt fix. Try to urinate on rocks or soil if possible. For aesthetic reasons, I also avoid peeing near or directly in streams unless I am on a desert river corridor where the recommended practice is to pee in the river. (Urine in the Western Hemisphere is pretty benign. In other parts of the world that is not always the case.)

Special Considerations for Special Environments

Desert, alpine and arctic regions, coastal areas, river corridors, and other special environments require some modifications to the minimum-impact techniques discussed earlier. It will require some judgment, research, and experience on your part to determine the best technique for a given area. Keep in mind that some practices are only suitable for remote locales. In areas of heavy use follow the regulations of the managing land-use agency. Always practice techniques that limit your impact to other human users as well as the environment.

When traveling on a large river corridor in remote areas such as the Arctic and some deserts, it is often best to camp on gravel bars near the outer edges of riverbeds when the river is low. The exposed gravel and sand make an excellent durable surface for pitching the tent and setting up a kitchen. It's best to use a little caution and thought in the placement of your tent, because heavy rains could cause the river to rise quickly. It's also a good idea to move the kitchen to higher ground after use. Note that in desert areas where thunderstorms are likely you should avoid placing your camp in washes and other flash-flood zones. Flash floods give very little warning and can be deadly, and the thunderstorms that cause them can occur far enough away that you might not even be aware of what's going on.

In coastal areas the use of a tide chart can help you choose a camp on the beach that will remain above high tide. If driftwood is plentiful, and you choose to have a fire, do it below the high-tide mark and the ocean will take care of it.

Regarding poop: In some circumstances—such as in remote/pristine arctic, alpine, and desert regions—it may be impossible to dig a cathole due to rocks and/or frozen soil. In these circumstances, it may be better to "smear" your dump (also known as "surface disposal.") This should only be done if the chance of another human coming by is slight to nil. Carefully pick a site 200 feet or more from any possible water sources (even dry ones) and scatter, or smear, your poop thinly. The sun and weather will break down the material and help to sterilize it. Pick a spot that will receive a maximum amount of sunlight, which dries the poop out and helps speed decomposition. By smearing the dump thinly out over the surface of the ground you also lessen the impact caused by digging in fragile soils.

On the ocean's shore, leaving poop well below the most recent high-tide line is often the best method for ensuring quick decomposition. The ocean is very good at absorbing and breaking down small amounts of organic waste quickly. Choose a site where the wave action is the greatest for best results. (Only leave human waste above the ground where the chance of another human being happening by is extremely low.)

Sometimes the best method for dealing with human waste is simply to carry it out. Certain places require you to carry your waste out in special bags or tubes due to the number of recreationists. The environment can absorb only so much waste. Areas like Mount Hood in Oregon now require climbers to pack out their waste. Boaters on popular multiday rivers routinely pack out their human waste. Check the regulations of the place you are headed to.

TRIP PLANNING

Any worthwhile expedition can be planned on the back of an envelope.

H. W. Tilman

There is a definite knack to planning a trip. Some folks need to work out every detail down to the finest minutiae. Others just throw it all together in a helter-skelter fashion that makes one wonder if they will even find the trailhead. There are lots of ways to plan a trip; most involve only a little writing and a lot of consideration. This chapter is about those things you should consider on any trip, whether it's a weekend in the Poconos or a 60-day expedition across Labrador.

Goals

The first things to consider on any backcountry trip are your goals. Goals really help to define the entire trip. Sometimes you have a specific destination in mind that requires a single-minded focus, such as getting to the top of some mountain or completing the Pacific Crest Trail. Other times you may just be out to "look around" a beautiful place. Some folks do trips to hang out with friends, but if one of the friends is all hot under the collar to get to that awesome fishing lake 20 miles in on the first day, trouble awaits. By defining goals for a trip, you help alleviate the problems and frustrations that crop up when different folks want to do radically different things. Maybe you will be able to accommodate different sets of goals for a trip, or maybe you'll have to settle for two different trips. Either way, life is made much simpler by making sure everyone on the trip is on the same page. Successful trips are successes because everyone comes home satisfied they achieved what they wanted, and most importantly, had a good time.

Setting goals lets you strategize on the best way to achieve them. It also helps determine what to bring on a trip. Do you want to go light and fast, or are eating well and being comfortable hanging around camp more the style? Sit down with the group of people on your trip and touch on everyone's goals and expectations, find the common ground, and then define a goal or vision. The longer and more involved the trip, the more important this pre-trip meeting is.

You don't need to have one single purpose. While it helps to have one all-encompassing goal there can be other objectives within this. If you have a specific goal in mind you may want to consider some other secondary goals in case you complete the first one early, or are unable to complete it at all.

Whom to go with

Deciding whom you want to go with is as important as your goals. You may have a specific purpose in mind and are just looking for others who share that same aim. On the other hand, maybe you already have a group of friends, and the challenge is to find a trip that satisfies everyone's appetite. For me the best part of a trip is not so much the trip itself, but the people I'm with. Keep this in mind because you will discover the truth in this as well.

In college, I remember my most frustrating times were planning a trip with friends, only to have them bail at the last moment. The best way to assure people's commitment to a trip is to get some money out of them. If partners are unwilling to lay down a little cash up-front—to pay for gas, food, or

NICE TEAMMATE
returning from a
water run for
everyone at once!

equipment—then they probably aren't that committed to the trip. Be it $10 or $500 (depending on the scope of the journey), a financial stake makes all the difference. This is especially true of any trip that has significant financial costs up-front. Figure out a budget for the trip and then have everyone who wants to go chip in around 20 percent of the total. A budget will also let folks see if it's affordable for them. This can help alleviate some potential stress down the road.

Making sure everyone is on the same page in terms of goals and commitments for a trip also gives you some insight into the compatibility of your team. We are all individuals with our own quirks and idiosyncrasies, and that's fine. In any walk of life you have to be understanding of the differences that exist between people. But if someone is way out of line with the norms of your group then it's better to get this resolved early on, rather than have to deal with the consequences later. It could mean something as minor as defining appropriate norms for everyone on the trip (such as no nudity) and getting each individual to agree to this. It might mean asking someone not to come along. I know I would be reluctant to join a trip if I felt way out of whack with the other people on it.

Lastly, any group needs leadership. It doesn't have to be autocratic leadership, but it's nice to know whom to turn to should the shit hit the fan. A leader helps when decisions need to be made quickly. It's also nice to have someone who facilitates decisions and steps in when needed. The leadership needed is usually pretty casual and by consensus most of the time, but having someone there to pick up the reins is reassuring. Keep this in mind when deciding on a leader: while it helps if their technical skills are good, they also need to be someone the group respects as a person.

Research

At some point in your planning you need to ask yourself if what you are hoping to do is realistic. Are there enough days planned to cover the mileage without the trip becoming a death march? Does the group have the necessary skills to overcome the expected hazards? Ask yourself some questions and do some research on the area you are planning to visit. Remember the rule of the 6 P's: Prior Planning Prevents Piss Poor Performance.

Places to look for information include guidebooks, the Internet, libraries, outfitters, retailers, public land managers, and folks who have been wherever it is you're going. Guidebooks can tell you a lot about an area or nothing useful at all. Hopefully they give you at least a little information that lets you plan a quality outing. Find guidebooks at local retailers. Lots of times only a retailer near the area you want to go will have a particular guidebook, but it's worth looking around until you find the one you want. The Internet can also help you look for guidebooks. Check out the on line bookstores or libraries.

If you're web surfing, search for the land agency responsible for the place you want to go—this often turns up some useful information. You can also search for the name of the place. The website called recreation.gov may also provide leads to the specific place you would like to go, or, if you're unsure exactly where you want to go in the first place, it could help you locate an area to do a trip. The web is a good place to look up international information as well, although it may not all be in English. If nothing else, your search might just turn up the phone number, e-mail address, or name of a land agency you can contact for more information.

Locating outfitters or retailers in the area of your trip is another thing that can be done by searching the web. Call the local chamber of commerce (get the phone number via the operator, or look on the web as most chambers have sites) and ask them to send you information. Never be afraid to call around and ask questions. Most people love to help out. If you get lucky, your search will lead you to someone who has been in area you wish to go. They may have even done a similar trip to the one you are planning. My experience has been that these people are the best source of information you can ever get about a place. I have gotten very detailed information from folks with firsthand knowledge of the area, and have been very grateful to them. Don't overlook these resources!

Permits and regulations

Important things to keep track of, in this age of increasing regulations and restricted access, are the specific rules of the land-managing agency that oversees the area in which you are planning to do your trip. In many places, like it or not, you are required to have some type of permit. Hopefully this has more to do with protecting the solitude of the place than with making money. Even if there are no permits involved, most areas have special regulations designed to protect the resources. These might include specific bear-camping practices, the restricted use of fires, human waste disposal practices, or use of designated campsites. You need to know about the regulations beforehand. It's disappointing to show up somewhere and find you lack a permit or are restricted to certain campsites that don't fit in with what you had planned.

What is the area like?

Ask yourself these types of questions:

- What is the bug factor?
- How hard is it to find water (especially in dry areas)?
- Are tents essential or can you get away with a tarp?
- How many people are you likely to see?

If headed to the mountains, find out how long the snowpack lasts into the summer. You may decide that a trip planned for May needs to be put off until late June. That or bring snow-shoes and/or an ice axe (learn how to use it first, of course).

Weather

The weather factor is twofold. One, find out what the typical weather is for the time of year you want to be there. While the weather is rarely "typical," it will still help you plan what you want to bring. You may even decide to change the timing of your trip based on this info. Two, get a weather forecast before you go. For weekend trips this can be really helpful and even accurate at times. Besides local radio or TV there are tons of good places on the web to get forecasts. For the adventurous surfer try weather.gov and follow the hyperlinks.

Potential hazards

Are bears or snakes a problem? Any other animals to watch out for? Will you need to do big river crossings or are there plenty of bridges? Are late afternoon thunderstorms and associated lightning common? Any bandits, guerrillas, or kidnappers to avoid?—don't laugh, this could be a problem if you are looking at an international trip. Knowing the potential hazards helps you plan your trip to minimize the risk.

You could also find out from land managers or local law enforcement agencies if car break-ins are common at your trailhead. This possibility probably exists at all trailheads, but some can be a lot worse than others.

Getting there

For a trip that starts and ends in the same place, just hopping in the car and following the road map may be all there is to it. Other times it can be more difficult—especially if it involves shuttles or public transportation. It's well worth your time to research this. In some cases it could lead to a change in plans. There's nothing worse than being unable to do a trip because you couldn't get to the trailhead. Hitchhiking is sometimes a good option, but in other places it's a study in patience, and best avoided.

Exchanging cars with another group of friends hiking in opposite directions can be a great way to shuttle vehicles around. They start at the roadhead you want to end up at and vice versa. I have some friends who saved a bunch of money once by splitting the cost of a flight into a remote part of the Arctic with another group who was flying out the same day. Money spent on phone calls to people you have never met might be well worth the effort.

Spots of interest

While you're doing all this research and talking to so many people, find out if there is anything on your route that is a must-see. Wouldn't you hate to get home and find out you'd missed a visit to some hot spring that was just around the bend?

Dogs

While a dog can provide entertainment and companionship, they can also be a nuisance and a threat to wildlife or other campers who may be canine-a-phobic. Folks who absolutely can't leave their pet at home should plan on the following:

- Bring a leash so you can restrain your dog should the need arise.

- Keep the dog in sight so you know it isn't out chasing wildlife or munching on some other camper's trail food.

- Make sure you can control your dog's barking. Barking dogs are a disturbance to others.

- Pooper scoopers aren't just for city parks anymore. If your pet defecates on the trail or in a campsite, pick it up, take it 200 feet away from any water source, and bury it. Either that or pack it out. Contamination of water sources comes from fecal matter in general, not just human waste.

HANDS FREE
light at night
techniques

- If your dog goes absolutely ballistic at the site of horses, deer, or other hikers, etc., leave it at home or keep it restrained at all times. Wildlife has a hard enough time without being harassed by dogs.

Now don't get me wrong—I love to pet dogs, throw sticks to them, and watch them chase their tails. As a former dog owner I understand the special relationship that forms between a pet and its owner. But dog owners need to be aware that not everyone loves their special companion as much as they do. In some places, such as national parks, it is illegal to even bring a dog hiking. Check out the regulations before bringing Fido with you.

Equipment Considerations

There is nothing more comical than watching someone try to set up a tent they have never used. However, it's better that this comedy takes place in the yard at home rather than during a downpour in the forest. This applies to all your gear from stoves to gaiters. Play with it at home first, before taking it camping. Looking over the gear at home will also give you an opportunity to make sure it's all there and in good repair. Nothing worse than finding out the first night of a ten-day trip that your stove's fuel line is broken, or that you left one of the tent poles behind. I know because both these things have happened to me—experiential learning at its best!

The next thing to consider about equipment is whom it belongs to. If you are doing a group outing with a bunch of friends, it's worth talking about what each person can contribute to the trip. No need to for each person to bring a first-aid kit or Leatherman. Figuring this out ahead of time lets you save weight.

One good question to ask is how you will share expenses if you need to purchase some expensive group item. Will one person buy it and be the owner, or will you split the cost and attempt to share the item in the future? Another idea includes selling it at the end of the trip and dividing the money. Discuss how you will deal with the piece of group gear that breaks or gets left behind. This is especially true if it belongs to one person—do they suck up the whole deal or does everyone split the cost? When my car got broken into on one of my trips, we all shared the cost of repairs and lost items. Discussing this first and having an agreement can prevent hurt feelings and pocketbooks down the trail.

Food and Fuel

Since an army is always happier if it's well fed, planning the amounts and types of food is one of the hardest challenges on any trip. When planning rations, it's important to take into account people's appetites and their likes and dislikes. Nothing worse than having oatmeal on a trip, I say—but Mike of course loves the stuff. Somebody on your trip might be a vegetarian. So ask around and find out what folks want for food and what they absolutely abhor. It's also important to find out if anyone has any allergies to food as well. My friend Brad would die from anaphylaxis if fed trail food that contained nuts.

So how do you go about planning a ration? There are two basic ways I know of. One is to plan meal by meal and the other is to figure out the poundage of food needed to feed so many people for so many days, then stick this into a formula designed to tell you how much should be trail food versus how much should be breakfast foods versus dinner foods, etc. My experience is that for short trips of four days or less, planning by meal is easier. For longer trips I prefer bulk planning. Either way works so give them both a try.

Whatever you do, bring enough food. You can do low-calorie trips—I've certainly done my share of them—but you have to be psyched to be hungry. Normally you are shooting for about 3,000 calories per person per day. Light eaters on shorter trips can get by with less (approximately 2,500 calories) while big eaters may want to consider bringing more food (approximately 3,500 calories). Be careful about bringing too much food, however. Arriving back at the car with enough food to spend another day or two camping means you have been carrying an extra 2 to 4 pounds of unneccesary weight. I like to arrive at the vehicle with an appetite.

Finally, I like to rebag or repackage most of my food. Two-ply plastic bags you can tie a knot in work best. Zip-locked bags work fine for trips of short duration, but if the zip fails on a longer trip it can be a bummer. Rebagging your food gets rid of unnecessary packaging like cardboard and the stuff they use to seal food in for long-term shelf life. This stuff is bulky and does not reseal well, so get rid of it. It makes for less garbage to carry around. Buying food in bulk quantities helps avoid all this packaging in the first place.

Meal planning

The concept here is to figure out how many total meals you need and then make a menu of what you want for each day.

E-Z CUTTING BOARD!

pinky extend

Fresh Garlic

chop!

tiny knife

the lid of your EATING BOWL!

ONE GALLON
4 Quarts
(3.7 liters)

ONE LITER
(.946 Quarts)

EASY METRIC CONVERSION
ONE QUART
is pretty much
ONE LITER!

This menu can range from very simple to very extravagant depending on your cooking experience and goals for the trip. I have done short trips where I didn't bring anything that needed cooking; I've also planned more involved menus (see example). There are plenty of good cookbooks out there, so I'm not going to go into any specific recipes. My experience is that if you can make it at home, you can make it out there.

Freeze-dried meals are very popular items these days, judging from the amount of them sold in outdoor stores. My experience is limited with these, but there are both good and bad freeze-dried meals. Some can be quite tasty, but others are either too bland or too salty. Menu planning works well with these, but make sure they are enough to fill you up. I'm a big eater and I can eat a freeze-dried meal packet for two and still have to cook something else up for dinner. Freeze-dried meals are also expensive, and those of us on a budget just can't afford many of them.

One nice thing about meal planning is that you can break it up and spread the planning out among your hiking pals. Say you are doing an eight-day trip with four friends. If each of you plans and brings two days' worth of meals for four folks then the food is covered.

Sample 2-day menu

Day 1

- Breakfast—quesadillas (tortillas, beans, cheese, and salsa)
- Lunch—peanuts, chocolate bar, and pretzels
- Dinner—spaghetti, red sauce, parmesan cheese, onion and dried broccoli

Day 2

- Breakfast—hash browns, cheese, and onion
- Lunch—cheese and crackers, orange, candy bar
- Dinner—sweet and sour rice (cashews, raisins, tamari, brown sugar, vinegar, oil)

Miscellaneous

- Condiments—butter, olive oil, spice kit
- Drinks—hot chocolate and tea

Bulk food planning

For longer trips, bulk-food rationing is the way to go. It's easier than coming up with a menu each time and gives you lots of flexibility in what to cook. I also think it makes you a better cook. Plus, the experience gained buying and cooking with bulk foods makes meal planning easier. You get a better sense of how much pasta or rice (etc.) to bring.

An example of bulk-food planning would be a ten-day trip with some friends on the Pacific Crest Trail. Say there were three of you, all moderate eaters. You would probably want to bring 1.75 pounds of food per person per day (approx. 3,000 calories). This would give you 52.5 pounds of total food (3 x 10 x 1.75). Using the following chart you would get so many pounds in each category. Round each number to the nearest half pound. Adding up all the categories should give you 52.5 pounds total.

Dinner	52.5 x 22% = approx. 11.5 lbs.
Breakfast	52.5 x 20% = approx. 10.5 lbs.
Trail food	52.5 x 25% = approx. 13 lbs.
Cheese	52.5 x 12% = approx. 6.5 lbs.
Drinks/soups	52.5 x 14% = approx. 7.5 lbs.
Desserts/sugar	52.5 x 5% = approx. 2.5 lbs.
Butter or margarine	52.5 x 2% = approx. 1 lbs.
	total=52.5 lbs.

Note: *Pounds of food per day refers to the dry-food weight. Canned goods contain water, which considerably increases weight without adding calories. Keep this in mind when choosing foods.*

I like to bag food in 1-pound increments. This is just a familiar way for me to look at food when I am planning a meal since I usually cook 1 pound of pasta, for example, for three people. If you plan on doing lots of bulk-food planning, a kitchen scale that weighs up to 2 pounds in 1-ounce increments is a good investment.

Feel free to mix and match categories. The percentages and categories are used as guides and are not set in stone. If you don't like cheese, bring peanut butter or tempeh instead. Put the pounds from the dessert category into trail food if you are a habitual snacker and don't like the idea of baking brownies. I'm not much of a hot-drink fan and typically leave that behind in the summer. If the weather is going to be cool, I may bring some fresh foods like onions, carrots, and potatoes.

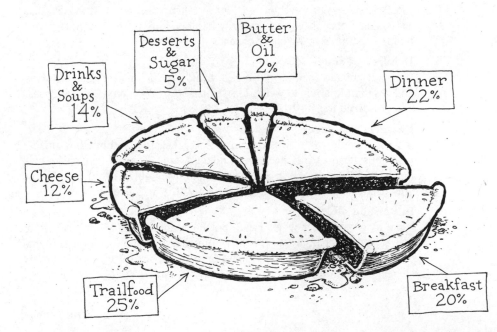

Bulk food categories

Below are some examples of the foods you might consider taking in the different food categories. You are certainly not limited to these, and while some people I know claim they could survive forever on hash browns and pasta, variety is the spice of life—not to mention nutrition, so bring a variety of foods to cover all the food groups. If you bring foods with long cooking times (such as brown rice or beans) you need to increase your fuel supply. Almost everything can be found nowadays in an instant form.

Dinner foods 22%
This category includes all the types of food you would want for dinner.

Examples: pasta, rice, beans, lentils, flour (for baking pizzas, biscuits, etc.) couscous, bulgur, instant potatoes, ramen noodles, tortillas, pitas, or other bread products.

Breakfast foods 20%
What do you like for breakfast? Bring it! I usually prefer the same types of stuff used for dinner, but other examples include cereal (both hot and cold), hash browns, bagels, English muffins, flour, or pancake mix (flour premixed with baking powder, salt, etc.).

Trail foods 25%
Trail foods are eady-to-eat snacks for the trail when you don't normally set up the kitchen for cooking. Some of this stuff (seeds, nuts, raisins) may be added to cooked meals.

Examples: nuts, seeds, dried fruit, energy bars, chocolate bars, cookies, crackers, hummus, cracker mixes, dried salami, or jerky. Check out the bulk food bins at your local grocer and have at it.

Cheese 12%
Lots of varieties here. Harder cheeses like parmesan and romano won't get as slimy in hot weather, but I have taken cheddar, jack, mozzarella, swiss, and cream cheese successfully in all conditions. Peanut butter and tempeh can be exchanged for cheese.

Drinks and soups 14%
Cocoa, lemonade or other powdered drink mix such as Tang, cider mixes and tea (don't bother to weigh tea), Cup-a-Soup, soup bases, sauce bases, and powdered tomato base.

Desserts and sugar 5%
Instant brownie, cake, gingerbread, cheesecake, jello, and pudding mixes. Also consider pre-made packaged cookie dough. Brown sugar packs better than white sugar. Hint: Save weight and bring only a little sugar if you only use it occasionally for tea or for activating and feeding yeast.

Butter and oil 2%
I like to bring butter when I can, but for long trips in warm weather it gets rancid faster than margarine. Double bag this and/or use a container with a screw-on lid to avoid leakage in your pack during hot weather. Oil can be substituted here, as well.

Since this food still has its water, I bring it in addition to my planned ration weight, although I will drop a pound or two of something else to save my aging back.

Don't necessarily limit yourself to 1.75 pounds of food per person per day. There may be times when you want 2 pounds per day or even 2.5 (a wintertime ration). This is especially true if you are all big eaters or are traveling during a cold time of year when your body needs more calories to stay warm. On the other side of the coin, there are times when 1.5 pounds of food per person per day is appropriate. The nice thing about bulk rationing is you can change the amount of food you are bringing. Even better, you can change the percentages of food. If you are finding 22 percent is not giving you enough dinner foods and you are consistently over on the amount of hot drinks you have for a trip, then reduce the percentage of hot drinks and add it to dinner foods. By playing around with the numbers and types of food you bring, you eventually fine-tune your system.

If you are still curious about bulk-food planning and would like some more resources, *NOLS Cookery* (see Appendix B) has an excellent section about ration planning as well as recipes, cooking tips, and other useful tidbits—not to mention more of Mike's freakishly cutesy-wootsy illustrations.

Spice kits

Lastly you should think about what to bring in your food repair kit. I never count this as food weight because it's far too important. Small plastic bottles work well for each spice.

Bring whatever spices you prefer, but for those who are wondering, the contents of my spice kit include:

garlic powder	curry	soy sauce or tamari
cayenne powder	salt	Tabasco
oregano and basil	cinnamon	vinegar
brewer's yeast	cumin	olive oil

You can also include your favorite dried vegetables to add taste and color. I love bringing dried broccoli and sun-dried tomatoes. Fresh garlic and ginger are also treats. Never sell yourself short on your favorite spices; simply adjust the amounts for the length of trip you have planned.

Rerations

For long trips, when you can't carry all your food (12 or more days for most folks) you need a way to resupply your food. There are a variety of ways to do this, from simply picking it up from a vehicle somewhere along your route, to having it flown in. This is where a little research with someone who has done the trip before really pays off. In some places you may have to use an airplane to get your rations in to you (Alaska for example). Not the cheapest option. In other spots, horse-packers can be hired to bring your reration to a certain spot at an appointed time (many trips in the Rockies are resupplied this way). The simplest way to do a reration might be to hike out to a road and pick it up from a vehicle. You could have someone meet you or have stashed the reration close by beforehand. Another similar alternative—one often used by folks hiking the Pacific Crest Trail or the Appalachian Trail—is to have your reration mailed to towns along your route. You simply hike out of the mountains for a day, pick up the food from the post office and head back in (a shower and a hot meal might also be in order). Just have a friend or relative mail the food to that post office, addressed to you and noted as "General Delivery," a week or so before you plan to be there.

(example address:)

JOE SHMOE
Appalachian Trail
Thru-Hiker
% GENERAL DELIVERY
Lyme, NH 03768

MAILING RERATIONS

REMEMBER:
FedEx & U.P.S.
Won't deliver
to a
GENERAL DELIVERY
ADDRESS!

Fuel

For white gas or other liquid fuel stoves, one-third to one-fourth of a quart per day for three people should be about right. Of course you can fine-tune this according to how efficient your stove is, how much cooking time is spent on the stove, and what time of year is it. In the late fall or early spring you might be making more hot drinks.

Leave some room at the top of your fuel bottle so the fuel has room to expand on a hot day or as you go up in altitude, otherwise it might leak out. Filling to about an inch from the top is good. Also leave room in the stove's fuel tank. This allows you to add pressure to the tank without over-pressurizing it. Leave about one-sixth of the tank empty.

Butane stove users should count on one cartridge per three days for three people. You should always bring an extra one, though, in case of a leak. And since it is hard to measure how much fuel is in the cartridge from your last trip, you may want to take another extra.

Maps

You can find topographic maps at most outdoor retailers. They should have maps of the local area and maybe more. If you are interested in other areas, they may also be able to help you locate a source for the maps you want. I would recommend starting with local sources as there is less running around that way.

If local leads aren't getting anywhere or don't have the maps you are looking for, then it is time to start looking at other sources. You can order maps direct from the USGS (United States Geological Survey). Ask for a free "state map index" if you are unsure of which maps you need (their website features an index as well). Popular hiking areas may also have commercially made maps that are water resistant and fairly detailed. Don't overlook the Forest Service, National Park Service, or Bureau of Land Management either, as they often have maps that—while not as detailed as a topo map— make for a good overview of the area you are going to visit. It is more informative to contact the local government office in the area you want to go. They may also be a good source for the topo maps in their area (or be able to give you the names of the ones you are interested in). Libraries are an excellent resource.

Map sources

There are many more resources than these, and with technology changing all the time, some of these links may or may not fit your needs. But it is a start at least.

Government
United States Geological Survey (USGS)
Box 25286
Denver, CO 80225
800-872-6277
www.mapping.usgs.gov

National Park Service (NPS)
NPS Room 1013
Washington, DC 20240
202-208-4747
www.nps.gov

US Forest Service (USFS)
14th and Independence Ave. SW
Washington, DC 20250
202-205-1760
www.fs.fed.us

Bureau of Land Management (BLM)
Office of Public Affairs
1849 C Street Rm 406-LS
Washington, DC 20240
202-452-5125

Commercial
Trails Illustrated
PO Box 4357
Evergreen, CO 80437
800-962-1643
www.wildfur.com/trails/trailhead.html

Earthwalk Press
2239 Union St.
Eureka, CA 95501
800-828-6277

Topozone
This website has all USGS topos available for view and download.
www.topozone.com

International
Canada Map Office
615 Booth St.
Ottawa, Ontario K1A 0E9
613-952-7000
www.maps.nrcan.gc.ca

Omni Resources
PO Box 2096
Burlington, NC 27216-2096
800-742-2677
www.omnimap.com

Emergency Planning

"What would I would do if _____." Thinking like this helps you plan for contingencies. What would I do if I got lost, or what would I do if one of my hiking partners gets injured? You can't always think this way or you will go crazy, but it does give insight into gaps in your knowledge. It's essential to know your options if someone were to get injured or lost on a trip. In such a case you usually contact the local sheriff's office or federal land manager, because they are the ones who initiate search and rescue operations. Know where the nearest phone is, and know if a cell phone (please, not for personal calls) or radio works in the spot you are headed. Simply dialing 9-1-1 is a good place to start. Consider carrying an overview map of the entire area you are hiking in along with a topo or trail map—this can give you useful information about surrounding areas including towns and roads. This is also important should you ever decide to bail on your planned route.

I always give a trusted friend a complete itinerary of my trip. This assures someone will come looking in the right spot if I don't return at a prearranged time. Giving it to a friend I trust to actually check up on me is an important part of the equation. I like to give them an estimated time of return, as well as a "freak time." The estimated time is when I am planning on returning. However, if I don't show up by this time, I don't want my friend mobilizing the National Guard on my behalf. After all, maybe I'm just a bit behind schedule due to a wrong turn or a late morning start. I might have just stopped for dinner on my way home. The "freak time" is the time I would actually like people to start looking for me. It can be hours or days from my estimated return time, depending on the length of trip.

If you do a solo trip, giving your itinerary to a friend becomes doubly important. There won't be anyone around to help out should you get hurt, so you really want to know someone will come looking for you. It is also important to stick to your planned route. One mishap in a place off your planned route could really extend and complicate a search. If you want to keep some options open on your trip, you can always include them on your itinerary. The same goes for bailout options. It would help should the unforeseen and undesired happen.

A treatment of backcountry first aid is really beyond the scope of this book. There are plenty of good wilderness first-aid books out there and I would recommend bringing one along, especially on long, remote trips. They make for interesting reading, especially when you have some medical problem to figure out. In addition, I would encourage anyone who plans to spend much time in the outdoors to take some type of first-aid or wilderness first-responder course.

While it is important to seek help if you really need it in an emergency situation, I also believe that self sufficiency is becoming a lost art these days. Too many people ignore it in our technological age since we have become conditioned to rely on others. I encourage you on all your trips to think— about how you would help yourself out, how would you get out of trouble if you got in it? Don't rely on a cell phone and the resources of others. We all have something we would rather be doing than helping out the bozo who spent the night out in cotton shorts and a T-shirt, because he didn't bring a map or pay attention to what was going on around him. Be prepared when you venture into the outdoors, so you can at least attempt to help yourself or others out. Nobody minds helping those who help themselves.

Putting It All Together

Keep it simple. Otherwise it's overwhelming. Figure out what you need, figure out who is going to get it, and let each person go at it. This will keep one person from being over-whelmed. It also gives everyone on the trip a sense of ownership. Write down all the things that need to be accomplished (an envelope will work), assign each to a person, and then cross them off as they get done. Avoid getting bogged down in details. Flexibility is the key to planning and pulling off any trip. Understanding the options is more important than having every detail nailed down. My favorite trips are the ones with the simplest logistics and the least dependence on technology.

OUTDOOR HAZARDS

Nothing you do in life is risk-free. Venturing into the outdoors carries with it a certain amount of risk. The more aggressive you are about what you choose to do on your trip, the more risk. There is nothing wrong with taking these risks—in fact, taking risks is how you learn and grow. Life is risky. Whether you are crossing a roadway, taking an airplane flight, or enjoying the view from a peak, there is some aspect of risk you assume along the way. Nowhere on earth are you free from all risks. Even if all you did was stay home and hide out from the world, an earthquake could still get you.

While travel in the backcountry has its risks, you can minimize these by gaining an understanding of the hazards that exist. Once you understand the hazards you can take action to reduce the risks or avoid them altogether.

There are two broad categories of hazards: objective and subjective. Objective hazards are part of the environment. They include such hazards as lightning, rockfall, animal attacks, river crossings, etc. Subjective hazards are the things each person brings with them on a trip. They include complacency, lack of experience, overconfidence, carelessness, etc. "Human error" is the term used to describe subjective hazards after an accident.

Objective hazards pose a risk only when humans interact with them. When crossing a river you expose yourself to the hazards of the river. You reduce your exposure to these hazards by choosing the spot you intend to cross and the methods you will use to cross. Subjective hazards come into play if you misjudge the depth or swiftness of the current, lack the experience to choose a better spot, or rush the crossing. Accidents usually happen due to a combination of objective and subjective hazards interacting together.

Preparedness

It's sad to hear about campers who got into trouble because they were unprepared to help themselves out. Bringing a cell phone into the woods, while forgetting essentials such as a map or extra layers, is not being responsible. Expect the unexpected to happen—then, if you have prepared for it and taken a cautious attitude toward what you do or choose to bring, you can usually figure out a way to help yourself. However, there might come a time when you need help, and there's nothing wrong with that. Nobody can predict everything. But by being resourceful and prepared, you should be able to solve most problems and have to call on others only in rare circumstances.

Awareness of hazards is the first step in reducing or avoiding them. This chapter covers some of the hazards found in the backcountry, but it certainly can't cover them all. Nor can it cover all the possible ways to reduce risk. This is where your own personal learning and judgment come into play. Learn how to read a map; look at the weather and be realistic about what could happen. Learn some basic first aid and equipment repair. Troubleshooting problems is enjoyable—it builds confidence and self-reliance.

Don't be afraid to take risks, but take appropriate risks that build on your experience base. As you gain experience you can take different risks and push yourself a bit more. Remember the axiom "Live to wimp again." If you find you're not quite ready for something, you can always come back to do it later when the conditions are better. I can't tell you how many times I have bailed because the situation was beyond my skill level at that point. As I have gained experience, what was once a challenge is now par for the course.

When you choose to venture into the outdoors you are accepting a degree of risk. If you are not comfortable with a certain hazard, avoid it. Stay out of grizzly country if you don't like their position on the food chain. Avoid river crossings if they aren't your thing. Stay off snow slopes if you don't know how to travel on snow.

Finally, take responsibility for the risks you choose to take. Expecting someone else to bail you out the moment you get into trouble is bad style. Blaming someone else for your predicament is even worse.

Animals

My rule of thumb regarding animals is if it is bigger than me, leave it alone. Any animal, big or small, will defend itself when threatened, so give them plenty of space. Male moose, when in rut in the fall, can be especially aggressive. You don't want

HOARY
MARMOT
(Marmota caligata)

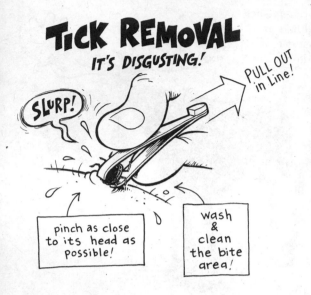

TICK REMOVAL
IT'S DISGUSTING!

SLURP!

PULL OUT in Line!

pinch as close to its head as possible!

wash & clean the bite area!

to surprise one of them on a trip to the privy.

In some places animals may carry diseases. Deer-mouse droppings and hantavirus are a serious health concern in parts of America. Rabies can also be a problem. I have a friend who was once attacked by a rabid cow in Baja, Mexico.

Ticks are another major carrier of disease. In tick country do daily checks of yourself looking for these little creatures. Think about wearing long pants with the cuffs tucked into a pair of gaiters. Long-sleeved shirts can be worn if lots of bushwhacking is expected. Remove ticks with a pair of tweezers up by their heads. Pull slowly out.

large straight gap

Long claws!

(front foot, approx 5 inches wide)

GRIZZLY BEAR

Small curved gap

Short claws

(front foot, approx 4 inches wide)

BLACK BEAR

Bears

If you plan to travel in bear country, there are certain precautions you need to take. It depends somewhat on the types of bears you are likely to encounter. Black bears tend to be the least aggressive of all the bears. This doesn't mean they won't attack you however, just that they are less likely. Black bears are far more common in the lower 48 states than any of the other bears. In some places they cause very few problems while in other areas they are downright pests.

Grizzly bears are more aggressive and unpredictable. They are more prone to attack if you enter their personal space, which may be anywhere from a few yards to a quarter mile. If you are in grizzly-bear territory, there are some very specific precautions to take, so read on. Both grizzly bears and black bears are omnivores, which means they eat a combination of food ranging from plants and animals to insects. Large mammals make up only a small percentage of their diets.

Polar bears are the worst in terms of aggressive behavior toward humans but are unlikely to be encountered unless you are hiking up near the Arctic Ocean or around Hudson Bay. They are very curious creatures with large appetites for warm-blooded creatures. If you encounter a polar bear, all bets are off. It may just be a fight to the death.

An encounter with any bear with cubs is a potentially dangerous and volatile situation. Mother bears with cubs are very protective of their young ones. They don't take kindly to

GRIZZLY
Ursus arctos

BOB HOPE "SCOOP" NOSE

SHOULDER HUMP

LOW RUMP

BLACK BEAR
Ursus americanus

STRAIGHT NOSE

TALL RUMP

strangers with cameras. If you ever encounter a cub, your best bet is to leave the area because Mom is almost certainly close by. If possible, go back the way you came.

Some general thoughts on bears

Bears do not normally seek out human interaction. While there have been a few cases of bears seeking out humans as prey, this is very rare, especially among black bears and grizzlies. In some places, however, bears have come to associate humans with food. While these bears may not be looking to

...with this technique you won't see ANY wildlife!

DING a LING!

munch on us, they would love whatever meals or snacks we may have in our backpacks or sitting around our camp. This sorry state of affairs has developed because of some people's sloppy camping practices and also because of poorly maintained garbage dumps, which have given bears easy access to human food and allowed them to associate human smells and presence with food. Bears who have come to think this way are referred to as "problem" or "habituated" bears and are often relocated or killed by land management agencies (ear tags may indicate that a bear is a problem bear). We can help reduce negative encounters between bears and humans by keeping food out of bears' reach, and packing out garbage from the backcountry so animals don't associate us with the grocery store.

Find out if the place you are headed for has any bear problems. Land managers can usually let you know what's up. If

Squint!

SNIFF!

Bears have poor eyesight & an excellent sense of smell!

you are headed to grizzly country, they can also tell you what the specific regulations for travel and camping are. In the lower 48 states you are required to either hang food or store it in bear-proof containers when in grizzly country.

The "safety in numbers" idea applies to bear country. Bear attacks are extremely rare on groups of four or more. Solo travel is by far the most dangerous. However, don't be lulled into a false sense of security just because you're hiking in a group. Some bears show no fear around groups of people, and unless you are all standing close together, a bear may not associate you with a group.

Bears are most active in the early morning and late evenings, so be more vigilant around those times.

Bears don't like surprises, and while a surprised black bear will most likely split the scene, a grizzly is less predictable. Hikers in grizzly country should make noise as they hike along. Clapping sounds, bad singing, and shouts warn bears that humans are on their way. Hopefully the bear will move along before you reach him or her. This is especially important if you are hiking in dense foliage or in undulating country where you might not see a bear until it is too late.

Bears do not appreciate dogs. While some hunters use packs of dogs to hunt down bears, the standard family dog is no match for a bear. Invariably a dog will try to chase a bear, infuriating the bear and causing it to turn on the dog. If the dog is not killed outright, it will run to you for protection with a very angry bear right behind it. Angry bears are to be avoided.

Lastly, keep an eye out for bear sign. Fresh bear tracks, scat, or other signs (i.e., clawed trees, torn-up logs, overturned rocks, or dug-up roots) indicate bears are in the area. In addition, food caches of dead animals should be avoided since bears will protect and defend their food. If you come upon a partially buried carcass or a spot that smells of decaying flesh, leave quickly. Staying alert for bears is your best technique to avoiding encounters with them. Paying attention to the wind direction will also help A bear that is upwind of you is not going to smell you and the sound of your voice will not carry as far either. Hike a little more cautiously going into the wind.

Bear encounters while hiking

If you happen to run into a bear while hiking, there are several things you should do. If the bear has not seen you, you should back off quietly and see if you can make a wide detour around the area. You can also wait until the bear moves off of its own accord and then move on. If the bear has seen you,

always be thinkin' about
WIND DIRECTION in BEAR COUNTRY

slowly back away until you are out of sight and can leave quickly. If it is close enough to hear your voice, speak to it in a firm but calm voice as you back away. Your goal is to help the bear identify you and let it know that you are not a threat nor are you prey. If need be, wave your arms slowly to help the bear with this identification.

Whatever you do, never run from a bear. Doing this could cause the bear to assume you are prey and trigger its predator instincts. With a speed of up to 40 miles an hour, a bear will quickly run you down. Screaming, looking a bear in the eye, and making quick movements can also set a bear on you, so refrain from these actions as well.

If a bear follows you, try dropping something (a bandanna, a hat, but not food!) to distract it while you continue to move away. People talk about climbing trees, but unless there is enough distance between you and the bear, you may not be able to climb high enough and quick enough to escape the bear. Bears are also capable of climbing trees, especially black bears but even some grizzlies, so you may have to climb quite high to discourage the bear.

Outdoor Hazards

Charging bears

If a bear charges you, there are a number of things you should do. While this advice may sound crazy, in most cases it's actually been shown to work. Keep in mind, most bear charges are just bluffs. They will either run by you or stop and back off. The bear is probably just as scared as you. Remember, running or turning your back to a bear is a bad idea.

If a bear stands upright it's probably only trying to see (and smell) you...

DON'T PANIC!

- Stand your ground. If you are in a group, you will all want to stand together, waving your arms and talking firmly. The idea is to convince the bear you are too big to attack. You don't want to threaten or provoke the bear further. Just convince him or her you mean no harm. If by yourself or in a small group (less than four), reduce your presence by standing sideways to the bear. Don't cower but keep quiet and still.

- Spray the bear with pepper spray if you have it. This will be most effective if you wait until just before the bear comes into range. The sound and sight of the spray as it comes out of the canister may be enough to scare the bear off. It will also require the bear to run through the cloud of spray to get to you. If the bear doesn't stop, give it a good dose right in the eyes. Attempt to back off again as the bear retreats or tries to rub the pepper spray from its face.

- In a worst-case scenario the bear will actually attack you. In this case your response depends on the species of bear. With a grizzly bear your best bet is to drop to the ground as the bear makes contact. While it may be tempting to drop sooner, this could turn a false charge into a mauling. You want to lay face down with your legs apart and your arms covering your head and neck. This will protect your vital organs and make it difficult for the bear to turn you over. In most maulings the grizzly will usually swat and bite you a few times before moving off. Wait until you are sure the bear has left the area before getting up, or you could trigger another attack.

- With a black bear, your best bet is to fight back if it attacks you. Try to punch and stab it in the eyes or nose. The same is true of a grizzly or polar bear that has decided you are its meal.

The good news about bear attacks is that they are rare; you are more likely to get stung by bees, bit by a snake, or attacked by a dog. This doesn't mean you shouldn't take precautions, though.

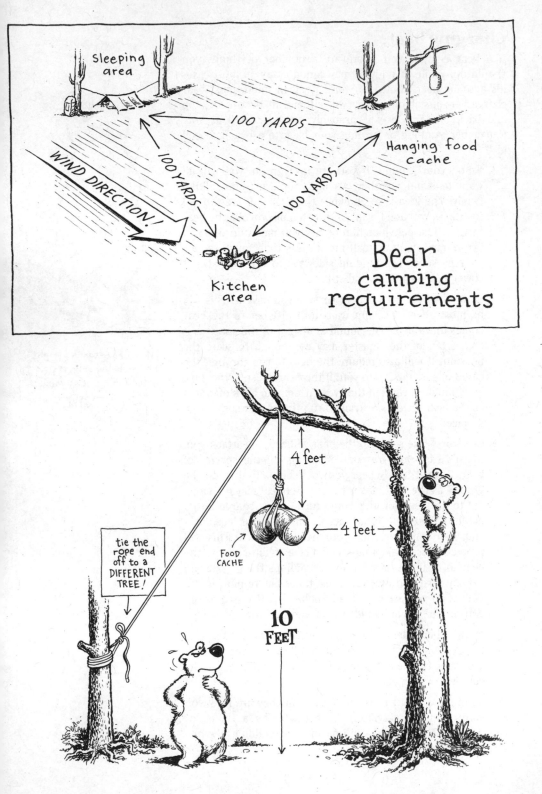

Pepper spray

In 1986, Bill Pounds marketed an aerosol spray made from hot peppers. The idea was that it would repel bears and be easier than a gun to use. The idea worked. Studies by some Canadian researchers showed it had an 85-percent success rate (as opposed to a 50-percent success rate for guns) in turning back aggressive bears. It is easy to use and carry and has become the accepted norm among backpackers in bear country.

Things to keep in mind about pepper spray:

- It has a short range, about 15 feet.
- If you are spraying it into the wind, look out; it'll come back in your face.
- Keep it handy; use a holster and attach it to the waist belt of your pack.
- Use a spray that contains between 1 and 2 percent capsaicin and related capsaicinoids or is EPA certified against bears. Don't expect those small, key-chain-type cans of pepper spray to work on a bear.
- Pepper spray works to repel bears only when sprayed in close contact with them. Bears are actually attracted to the smell of the residue. So don't go around spraying yourself or your campsite.
- Airlines and customs officials may not approve of your carrying pepper spray. Find out the regulations ahead of time.

BEAR HANG using simple **PULLEY!**

a. THROW! Rock!

b. knot w/loop — knot — carabiner — FOOD BAG!

c. biner as PULLEY — TIED OFF — PULL! — mechanical advantage 'BINER — HEAVY!

SIMPLE **2to1** PULLEY SYSTEM for getting the big load off the ground.

Bears and camps

Besides knowing what to do to avoid bears on the trail, it's essential to know how to discourage them in camp. Hanging food and camping away from your kitchen are part of the equation. There are a number of ways to hang food (see illustrations), but the important thing to remember is your hang must be at least 10 feet high and 4 feet from tree trunks and all branches. Even this won't discourage some bears, but it helps in most cases.

A bear hang will do no good unless you use it. Keep all food, spices, garbage, toothpaste, sunscreens, and other fragrant items in your food hang. Some people will even cook in their wind clothes and then leave them in the bear hang. Don't leave your food unattended on the ground. Hang it when not in use.

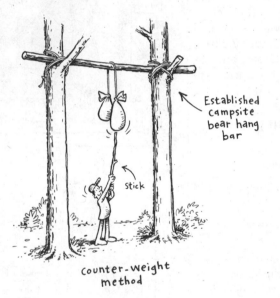

← Established campsite bear hang bar

stick

Counter-weight method

Bear canisters are useful for places where there are no trees to hang your food. The tundra in Alaska, for example, has lots of bears but no big trees for hanging food. Canisters are shaped in such a way that bears can't open them or carry them off. Denali National Park will actually issue you a bear container with your backcountry permit.

You want your food hang and kitchen to be at least 100 yards from camp. Preferably camp is uphill and upwind so food smells don't drift through your tent. Never snack around your campsite as food smells could linger there. Keep all odorous things (with the exception of your tentmates) in the kitchen.

Equipment for bear hangs

5mm to 6mm perlon rope: one or two of these ropes between 30 to 60 feet in length, depending on your style of hang and the weight of your food.

Carabiners: two or three of these can be useful as pulleys or attachment points.

Small stuff sack: useful for getting the rope over a branch. Fill with rocks or dirt, tie to the rope, and toss away.

9 feet of webbing: can be tied around a tree as the anchor for a 3-to-1 pulley system.

Food bag: any nylon bag that can be attached to a rope. Zippered duffel bags work great for this.

Other things to consider in bear country:

- Sleep in your shelter. While those nylon walls may seem pretty thin, they do offer a barrier, if only for camouflage.

- Keep your bear spray with you around camp and in the tent. If it has been discharged, wash it to remove the odor from it.

- Don't place your camp or kitchen on game trails.

- Put your kitchen in a place where you have a good field of view. If camping in more than one group, keep the kitchens in one area and the camps together in another area. Avoid spilling food, and sump all wastewater in a hole in the ground or into a large stream. I like to wipe my dirty, greasy hands on a bandanna rather than on my clothes. The bandanna stays with the food bags and gets hung up. Wash up when done cooking.

BEAR HANG
(TWO TREE HAULING TECHNIQUE)

- Trips to the bathroom should be done in pairs or close to camp. Make plenty of noise and take your bear spray.

Bears in camp are bad news. Hopefully, they are just curious and will move on. In large groups I will get everyone together to see if that will discourage the bear. Making a lot of noise may help drive a bear off. If the bear doesn't want to leave, then you may have to leave. I have never had a standoff with a grizzly in camp, although I have had a few pass through.

If I was in a small group (less than four) I would either leave the scene quietly, climb a tree (at least 10 feet high if not higher), or hide out in the tent with the pepper spray, depending on the situation. Hopefully the bear is only after the cocoa.

With a black bear you can be a little more aggressive (especially in a group). In my experience you can make lots of noise, throw things at it, and try to run it off (don't do this with a grizzly). If it persists in hanging around, it may be time to move on, with or without your gear.

Any bear that acts aggressively or attacks in camp is thinking "dinner," and the main entree is you. Your only choice is to escape or fight back with all your means.

Getting Lost and Staying Found

Patrick McManus writes an exceedingly funny piece about getting lost in his book *A Fine and Pleasant Misery*. In reality, getting lost isn't all that fun, and while I have never truly been lost, I have been disorientated a few times. What to do all depends on your situation, but here are some general guidelines.

If you are disorientated as a group or as an individual hiking alone, your goal becomes one of relocating where you are so you can proceed to your destination. Try climbing to a high point where you can see the lay of the land. This may allow you to locate yourself on a map. Take the time to figure out where you are as soon as you feel you're disoriented—it saves a lot of unnecessary travel. I will also scout around if this helps me locate features that tell me where I am. Be careful while scouting that you don't become separated from your companions or gear. If this happens, being lost takes on a whole new dimension.

It may be best to stick together and keep your gear with you. If this doesn't help, then try to retrace your steps till you orient yourself again. As a last resort you can pick one of two options.

1) Attempt to hike out to a road. Roads lead to towns. It won't be the shortest or easiest solution—the nearest road could be a very long ways away with lots of challenging off-trail travel—but it works. In the mountains all streams flow out to the flats, and unless you are near the ocean they are invariably crossed by a road. All trails eventually hit a road as well. Pick the direction you think is heading out. In flatter country pick a direction and stick to it. Eventually it will lead to some human-made feature. (This works best in areas that are surrounded by roads, which is usually the case in the continental U.S. In places with large tracts of undeveloped country, such as northern Canada, your best bet will be to relocate yourself, wait for help, or go the distance in a cardinal direction [north, south, east, or west] it takes to find a road.)

2) With the above option you run the risk of getting so far off your planned route that a search and rescue team might never find you. You might be better off staying in one place, especially if you left a "freak time" and itinerary with some friends. In this case make yourself as visible as possible. Lighting a big, smoky fire is appropriate if the possibility of starting a forest fire is low. A mirror can be used to flash any planes flying overhead on a sunny day.

Getting separated from your hiking partners is a slightly different story. Your goal should be to find them, or better yet, wait for them to find you. Try to retrace your steps, scout around some, and go to a high point. If you still can't figure out where you are and yelling doesn't locate the group, then make yourself visible and stay put. This will make it easier for your group to find you. Make yourself comfortable. If it looks like you will spend the night without a shelter, then build a fire for warmth if you can. Otherwise, bivying under trees and using leaves and grass as insulation will help keep you warmer. Stay hydrated.

If you suspect a member of your group has become lost, then you will need to organize a search for them. While searching haphazardly may be the first strategy, it will be more effective in the long run to have a plan of action. First, figure out the point where the lost person was last seen. From here figure out the most likely place they would go. Most people will head in a downhill direction when lost. Open places will be more attractive to a lost person than dense forest.

Identify likely corridors of travel, such as trails, streambeds, canyons, or valley bottoms. From the place the person was last seen, send searchers out along these possible travel corridors to leave notes at the outer edges of your search (approximately 6 miles) telling the lost person to stay there. You will need to check these places periodically. Make an inner search area about 3 miles around the last place the lost person was seen. Search in this area first and then in the outer 6 mile circle. Take note of any clues you might find. If it looks like you are not going to locate the person soon, send out for help.

Staying found

It's much easier to identify landmarks that will keep you from getting lost than it is to figure out where you are after you're lost. Keep the following in mind:

- Use landmarks as handrails when hiking. Identify these handrails before you start each day and check them off as you go along. Keep track of where you are on the map. Don't convince yourself you are where you want to be on the map. Fit the terrain to the map by identifying five features around you then finding a spot on the map that matches these five features.

- Stay together while hiking. This way one person can't get separated from the group.

- When you make camp, locate some landmarks you can use to locate camp in case you wander away for some reason, i.e., to get water, take a dump, or go for a hike.

River Crossings

Crossing rivers is one of the more dangerous risks backcountry travelers face. While small creeks may not pose much of a hazard other than slick rocks and wet feet, a stream or river with enough water to wash you off your feet is another story. Unplanned swims and foot entrapment are serious risks that need to be recognized and avoided.

Scouting

The smartest move you can make before attempting any river crossing is to take a good look around. Scouting upstream and downstream is the best way to locate the safest place to cross. Sometimes it may only be a matter of a few yards—other times you may have to travel a few miles. In some places you need to travel upstream far enough that you cross several tributaries of the river you are attempting to cross. The more tributaries you cross, the less water volume in the river. At some point it should get easier to cross. It all depends on the situation. Ideally you are looking for a wide, shallow section of river where the current is slow and there are no downstream hazards such as strainers or rapids. The reality of finding such a perfect spot might be slim, but your goal should be to reduce as many of the hazards as possible.

On bigger rivers look for places where the river is braided. The multiple smaller channels are easier to cross, and gravel bars provide rest areas. It takes more scouting to find the best way across since you can't always see the entire river in one shot, and each channel may need to be scouted. But it may provide the only option.

If you must cross in a place where the water is deep and swift, then make sure there are no downstream strainers or holes to trap hikers should they swim. If crossing above such hazards is your only choice, then do so in slow-moving shallow water where the chance of swimming is low. This process of compromise and hazard reduction is how you lessen the risk.

Other things to look for when scouting include dry crossings and what the far side of the river looks like. If you have a great crossing that goes over to a steep, muddy bank, you may be stuck in the river. Check out the far side of your crossing carefully—how thick are the bushes, does the river get deeper next to the bank, etc. These are good questions to ask.

River hazards

Strainers: Downed trees, bushes, or logs that are in the water but also attached to shore so the water moves through, under, and over them. A person floating into a strainer becomes entangled and the force of the water holds the person against it. Avoid these at all costs! If unable to avoid floating into a strainer you should swim directly at it and try to climb up on it before the water pins or pulls you under.

Holes or hydraulics: Formed by rocks just under the water's surface. Holes cause the water to recirculate back upstream. Large holes can recirculate a person as well. Recognized by white, foaming water. A bigger danger to the swimming hiker probably comes from getting banged up by the rock forming the hole as he or she goes over it. The eddies behind small holes can sometimes be used in crossing as the current is not as strong here.

Rocks: These are slippery and can bang up the unsuspecting hiker. A foot caught under one can lead to a heads-down drowning situation. The force of water pushes you over and it becomes impossible to get back up. If you find yourself swimming in a river, do not attempt to stand up until you reach shallow water (below the knees).

Floating logs: If you are halfway across a thigh-deep river, imagine how bummed you would be to see a large log floating down toward you. On big crossings it may be wise to post someone upstream to warn of such hazards.

Cold water: Hypothermia is no joke. Even if you don't fall in the river, cold water can sap your strength. Be especially careful on cold, wet days or on long crossings. I will often wear my polypro bottoms in such cases to provide more warmth. They dry quick enough once the crossing is over.

FOOT ENTRAPMENT!

Dry crossings

Dry crossings sure are nice, but they become harder to find as the stream gets larger. Small creeks can be stepped or jumped across. Rocks protruding above the water's surface can be used as stepping stones to the other side, and downed trees sometimes form bridges across rivers. Be careful if the rocks or logs are wet. The wetter they are, the slicker they are.

When crossing from rock to rock plan your route ahead of time. It is easier to balance on a rock while in motion to the next one than to try to stand on it looking for the next rock. A stick or pole can also help provide balance while stepping from rock to rock.

Logs or log jams can make great places to cross and may provide the only dry crossing options on bigger streams. Depending on your sense of balance, the diameter of the log, and how slick it is, you may choose to walk across or shimmy across on your butt. Once again a pole can be useful for balance, although some log crossings may be too high or the water too deep for this to work. Multiple logs all jammed together often provide more security since you can spread your weight out between them and use different combinations of logs for balance. Watch for loose bark or rotted logs that can break under your feet, causing you to plummet into the water below. Also be careful with log crossings because the same logs that form the bridge become dangerous strainers if you happen to fall into the water. If your party is carrying a rope, a hand line can be created to help provide a little balance for crossing the log with a pack on.

HAND LINE

High-stepping

Semi-dry crossings

On smaller streams where no dry crossing presents itself you can sometimes get away with high-stepping across (see illustration). The idea here is that with good gaiters cinched snugly to the boot and quick steps designed to splash water away from your foot, you can cross with only the outsides of your boots and gaiters getting wet. This method requires the river bottom be relatively smooth (sand or small stones) so you don't stumble and/or tweak an ankle. The deeper the water and the longer the crossing, the less effective this method is at keeping you dry.

As soon as you are across shake your feet to get the excess water off them so it doesn't soak into your boots.

Wet crossings

Often the only way to cross a stream or river is to wade across it. In this case there are a number of factors to keep in mind:

- depth of the water
- speed of the current
- temperature of the water
- distance across
- what forms the river bottom
- what is downstream of you

All of these help determine how you go about crossing the river. Depth and speed of the water determine how much force the current will exert on you. The deeper and/or faster the current, the harder and more dangerous the crossing becomes. While it may be possible to cross a chest-deep river that hardly has any current, I have seen ankle-deep streams that were impossible to cross due to the speed of the water. If you are unsure about a crossing, first try wading across without your pack to see how it feels. Any crossing that is knee-deep or deeper has greater potential danger, due to the increased chance of swimming and/or foot entrapment. Keep this in mind and plan accordingly.

Wind pants and loose clothing make crossings harder because they catch the water and create more force against your legs. Remove such clothing if it is a challenging crossing. For really cold water, it is a good idea to wear long underwear. Long underwear is tight fitting and porous enough that it creates very little drag, and the extra warmth it provides outweighs the drag it does have—especially in long crossings or on cold days.

A long crossing is potentially more dangerous than a short one just because you are in the water longer. However, finding the widest spot in the river also means the river will be shallower than at a narrower spot. In general, the force of the current is less in a wide area, so the crossing should be easier.

River bottoms with medium-sized to large rocks make crossing more difficult and increase the possibility for foot entrapment. In really powerful rivers you may hear rocks rolling downstream on the river bottom. Avoid crossing at these places. Also pay attention to what is downstream of you. If there are hazards, you may decide to find a different crossing.

Strategies for crossing

There are a number of ways to go about wading a river depending on the severity of the crossing and number of people who need to get across. I can touch on some basic ideas and principles, but it would be impossible to describe all the different ways. Keep the following in mind:

- Cross looking upstream. This way you can always see what is coming at you.

- Avoid staring at the river—it can cause you to lose your sense of balance. Keep your eyes moving about or look at the banks.

- Sidestep across and don't cross one foot over the other. This keeps you in a better position of balance.

- Use a stick for balance. In swift current you can lean on this stick and create a tripod for increased balance. Move one foot, move the other, then move the stick.

Really lean into it!

THIRD POINT OF BALANCE (tripod)

The handholding CHAIN technique

- If the river is knee-deep or deeper, make sure pack waist belts and sternum straps are undone. This way if you happen to fall you can slip out of the pack quickly.

- Avoid crossing in areas with well-developed waves or downstream "V's" (where the water is constricted) as the currents here will be too strong.

I am in the habit of wearing my boots for river crossings. If there are a lot of crossings to be done, or my feet are wet from hiking in the rain, I don't even bother switching out of my socks. Why bother wasting time is my philosophy; let the water squish out of the boots as I hike along. Neoprene socks are really nice for this.

If I know this is my only crossing of the day, then I may decide to remove my socks and insoles and just let my boots get wet. If the crossing is challenging, however, I leave all this in place because boots without socks and insoles are really floppy, and I want my boots to support my ankles when I'm crossing. Gaiters can be worn for shallow crossings or in a mellow current, but for swift water they can add a lot of drag to your foot. However, gaiters are advantageous to keeping small stones and sand out of your boots. Some of these things you'll just have to decide for yourself.

CURRENT

4 PERSON OVER-VIEW

Some people prefer to do crossings in their camp shoes or in sandals. While this may be fine for mellow crossings, it really doesn't provide protection or support for more challenging crossings. My feet are very important to me in the backcountry, and getting my boots wet is no big deal.

River crossings can be made alone, in pairs, or in large groups, all depending on the situation. Find a safe spot in a river and experiment to decide what feels most stable. This is how you really learn about what you can do, and it lets you get a feel for different ways to cross.

the **TRAIN** technique

CURRENT!

Attentive SPOTTER!

Other thoughts on river crossings

Waist belts on or off? Some folks are of the school that keeping your waist belt on gives better balance, which means there's less likelihood of taking a dunk. While I can agree with this, I feel the danger of trying to unbuckle a pack while swimming greatly outweighs any advantage of leaving a pack buckled. Whether the crossing is dry or wet, I always unbuckle my waist belt and sternum strap if the water is deep enough to swim in.

Time of day can be important to your crossings. Snow-fed rivers may be higher in the afternoon than after a cold night. Waiting to cross when the river is lower may make the crossing more feasible. In the same vein, if it has been raining hard and you have an impassable river, waiting a day or two for the river to drop to a manageable level is the safest option. Lastly, consider your state of being. A hard river crossing done at the end of a long day will be more challenging than if you do it fresh the next morning.

In both dry and wet, crossings it is a good idea to "spot" people. This can mean as little as offering them a hand to actually setting yourself up (without your pack) downstream to help someone out of the water should they fall in.

THREE PERSON TRIPOD

Never be afraid to let someone else carry your pack across a river or choose a different crossing if you are uncomfortable with one. I have turned around and gone somewhere else when I have encountered nasty river crossings I didn't feel right about.

Should you ever have a rope to assist you in doing a wet crossing, always cross on the downstream side of it, and never attach a person to it.

Some deep, fast-moving rivers are impossible to cross without the aid of a boat. On a trip I once did in Chile we actually carried a small rubber raft for river crossings. On the other hand, I know people who have swum across slow-moving rivers either towing or pushing their packs. Good luck keeping stuff dry if you try this.

POSITION THE BIG GUY UPSTREAM

CURRENT

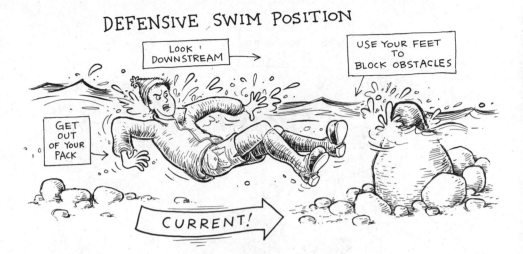

DEFENSIVE SWIM POSITION

LOOK DOWNSTREAM →

USE YOUR FEET TO BLOCK OBSTACLES

GET OUT OF YOUR PACK

CURRENT!

If you swim

Know what to do should you ever fall and swim during a river crossing. First, get rid of your pack. If you have spotters on shore, they can help recover the pack (it will float). If not you can try to swim with it, but this should be a low priority if there are any downstream hazards. After ditching the pack get in the defensive swimming position—"sit" facing downstream, feet forward to fend off obstacles—and take a look downstream. By doing the backstroke you can work your way to shore while using your legs to keep you off rocks. Be careful if you find yourself going over any holes—keep your head and feet up. Aggressively swim to shore as soon as you can; do the crawl stroke if necessary. You should also aggressively swim away from any river hazards. Don't attempt to stand up until the water is below your knees, or you run the risk of foot entrapment.

Flash Floods

In some areas flash floods are a problem. Typically, these are desert areas during the time of year when thunderstorms are common. But any place experiencing heavier than normal rain is also at risk. I once walked though an area that had been recently devastated when a glacial dam burst. No way to predict that. Look at your map to view the extent of an area drained by a creek or wash. This can give you an idea of its potential for flooding. The larger the upper watershed, the greater the potential. In canyon areas be careful of any thunderstorms in your area. While it may not be raining on you it

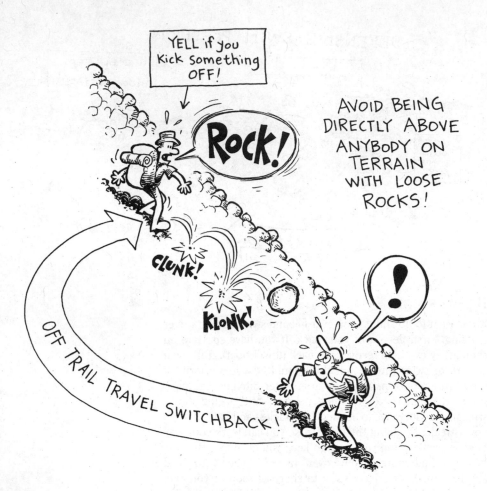

could be raining quite heavily at the headwaters. Avoid camping next to creek beds and below incoming drainages and hiking in slot canyons during heavy rains or periods of high thunderstorm activity.

Scree, Talus, and Boulders

Crossing fields of rocks is a challenge in itself. Balance, agility, and confidence all come into play. When the rocks you are crossing are on a hill or mountainside the danger of falling or rolling rocks needs to be considered. Pay attention to where the other members of your group are. Pick separate lines of travel that keep you clear of any rock your buddy might knock off from above. In really narrow confines, such as a gully where you can't spread out, stay right next to one another so a loose rock won't be able to generate any speed before it hits someone, or travel one by one to zones of safety out of the way of rockfall. Should you ever knock a rock loose yell "ROCK!!" so others can take cover or move out of the way. If you have a helmet, put it on.

Rocks that have been on the ground a long time tend to be more stable underfoot than ones that have fallen more recently. Look for moss or lichen growing on the rock. This is a sure sign the rocks have been there awhile and may have settled in more. Rocks free of vegetation and with recent signs of scarring indicate that lots of rockfall is still occurring. Be extra careful in these places and avoid loitering.

Try to step on the UPHILL side of each rock

DENIAL of GRAVITY

AAWK!

SKITTER!

mmm... pleasant

(GRAVITY)

(Boulder Field Drama)

Step on the uphill side of a rock. They tend to be more stable this way, and I would rather be on top of a rock that starts to move than under it. This way I can either step off it or "surf" it until it stops.

Boulders are any rocks too big to pick up; at least that's my definition. Some boulders are small enough that you can simply walk across the top of them, picking your route out as you go. In some cases you will want to move quickly across the tops of a few rocks to stay in balance and then pause to scope out your next move from a more stable platform. Other boulders can be so big that you are literally climbing among them, using both your hands and feet for balance and movement. I find boulder fields easier to go up than down. Less impact on the knees and easier to stay in balance.

The scariest thing about big boulders is loose boulders. Some of them will tip from side to side when you step on them, which can be a frightening feeling. But unless this causes you to fall they're probably not that dangerous. Big perched boulders are the scariest ones for me because they are the ones that could roll down a hill crushing anything in their path. I

Hardpan

avoid these like the plague. Shifting boulders are also scary—I would hate to get a hand or foot caught between two boulders. Most of the rocks in a boulder field will be relatively stable, but it pays to be on the lookout for the one that's not.

In contrast to boulders are scree and talus slopes. On this terrain none of the rock is very stable underfoot. Scree is the smallest of rocks, akin to gravel. Scree slopes are tedious, at best, to go up. It's like trying to walk up the down escalator—every step up comes down again in sliding rock. On the other hand, scree slopes can be quite fun to go down. It's like running down a sand dune. Take lots of quick steps with the heels dug in. Don't wait for your foot to come to a stop; just keep on sliding downward with each step.

Be sure that you really are on a scree slope and not on hardpan. Hardpan covered with small pebbles doesn't allow your heels to sink in. Instead, your foot will glance off the ground while the pebbles act like ball bearings. Desperate!

Talus slopes are the worst of both worlds. While smaller than boulders, talus is big enough that you don't want it sliding along with you. But like scree it tends to move underfoot making traction hard. The best strategy in talus is to move cautiously, being careful to step on the uphill sides of rocks and keeping each person clear of the occasional rock that starts rolling downward. The steeper the slope, the more dangerous loose rock is.

WEATHER

Weather is neither good nor bad, it simply is what it is. As humans we like to classify our relation to weather. If we want rain it's good; if not, it's bad. When we go camping we are making a decision to live with whatever weather event comes along. We don't get hypothermia from bad weather. We get it from dealing with the weather badly. This is why good camping skills are important.

When backpacking we can't hide from the weather by retreating at the first sign of rain. Weather, unfortunately or fortunately, does not lend itself to easy understanding. It is a complicated interplay of numerous variables and gets harder to predict the further away in time we try to forecast. In the backcountry, without access to the forecast from the National Weather Service or the local meteorologist, we can only guess at what is coming at us. But then again, that's kind of what weather forecasters do anyway.

COLD FRONT

With some knowledge about how weather works, we can at least make informed guesses. My goal here is to share some of my knowledge of weather and the things I consider when living under the stars. Jim Woodmencey's *Reading Weather* is an excellent treatise on the subject for more inquiring minds (see Appendix B).

The Basic Principles

WARM FRONT

Warm air holds more moisture than cold air. So when a meteorologist is talking about a warm front, he/she is talking about a mass of air that contains a lot of moisture relative to the other air masses around it. This is an important concept to grasp. Air masses are looked at and compared to one another on a relative scale. Not every warm front is the same, and each may have different amounts of moisture, be large or small, and so on.

Warm air is lighter than cold air. Because it is lighter it will rise whenever it can, such as when surrounded by cooler air.

As warm air rises it cools. If it cools enough, the moisture in it, in the form of water molecules, begins to condense into small water droplets. These small water droplets are what we view as clouds. If there is enough water vapor in the air mass and/or it continues to rise and cool, then the clouds get thicker and darker, and eventually the water droplets will grow big enough to cause rain or snow.

Air masses with lots of moisture are considered low pressure systems. This is because a given amount of moist air weighs less than the same amount of dry air. (This has to do with the molecular weights of water, oxygen, and nitrogen. All that stuff we should have learned in chemistry).

Areas of high pressure are relatively drier air masses. This is why when we are under a high pressure system, we are usually experiencing clear, sunny weather.

If a low pressure system encounters a high, it will rise up over the high pressure system because it is lighter.

A warm front occurs when a mass of warm air follows behind a mass of colder air. Warm fronts advance slowly. High, thin clouds build slowly, getting thicker and lower, eventually becoming rain clouds. While significant amounts of moisture may come from a warm front, they are less violent than shorter-lived cold fronts.

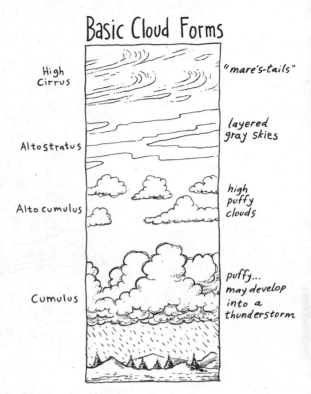

Basic Cloud Forms

High Cirrus — "mare's-tails"

Altostratus — layered gray skies

Alto cumulus — high puffy clouds

Cumulus — puffy... may develop into a thunderstorm

Cold fronts occur when a quick-moving mass of cold air wedges its way under a mass of warmer air. As the warm air is forced higher it cools, and the moisture condenses out quickly. This rapid lifting and cooling often produces violent short-lived storms. Lightning and strong winds are often the result of a cold front.

Orographic lifting is a local weather effect. When an air mass encounters a mountain range it is forced up over the range. This causes the air mass to cool rapidly and lose its moisture as it is being pushed up. Once over the crest of the range the now cooler dry air begins to sink. Since most weather comes from the west in the United States, it is typically the western side of a mountain range that experiences the most precipitation. The east side of the range sits in what is called the "rain shadow" and is typically drier as the air has lost much of its moisture. Many of the world's deserts sit in the rain shadow of some mountain range.

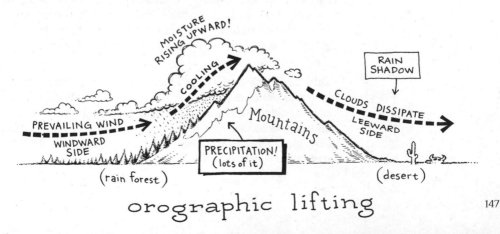

MOISTURE RISING UPWARD!

COOLING

RAIN SHADOW

CLOUDS DISSIPATE

PREVAILING WIND

WINDWARD SIDE

Mountains

LEEWARD SIDE

PRECIPITATION! (lots of it)

(rain forest)

(desert)

orographic lifting

INSULATION!

Lightning position.

Thunderstorms and lightning

The greatest threat to hikers from weather in the outdoors is lightning. A direct strike is almost always fatal, but you don't need to be struck directly by lightning to be affected—the electricity from a strike can also travel through the ground. The associated ground current dissipates with distance away from the strike but can be lethal or not depending on where you are in relation to it.

Lightning is a product of thunderstorms. Thunderstorms are a result of instability in the atmosphere brought about by the rapid rising of air. This rapid rising occurs when air at the earth's surface is heated by the sun at a rate faster than the air above can warm. This warm air then begins to rise quickly. Orographic features and cold fronts can accelerate the rate at which warm air rises, or they can create thunderstorms on their own.

This rapid rising of air produces the big, towering cumulonimbus clouds associated with thunderstorms. Within these clouds, violent updrafts and downdrafts strip the electrons off water molecules, creating electrical imbalances within the cloud and between the cloud and the earth. Most lightning strikes are cloud to cloud.

Thunder is a product of the rapid expansion and contraction of air caused by a bolt of lightning. Because light and sound travel at different speeds, you can estimate how far away lightning strikes are occurring. Count the number of seconds between when you see a flash of lightning and when you hear the thunder boom. Every five seconds you count represents 1 mile. So, a lapse of ten seconds between when you saw the flash until you heard the boom represents 2 miles. Time to look for cover!

The same goes if your friend's hair starts to stand on end or the hair on your face starts itching. Buzzing and cracking sounds also indicate electricity in the air. This comes from the buildup of ions in the area around you. The smell of ozone may also be in the air. The possibility of a strike is imminent, and you should look for cover instantly.

While the chance of getting hit by lightning is low, you can reduce this chance even more by taking certain actions. For one, stay off high ridges or peaks during a thunderstorm. Lightning wants to take the shortest distance from the cloud to the ground, so it is much more likely to hit up high than down low. For the same reason, avoid standing under the tallest tree around or in an open field. Lightning will seek the tallest object. Golfers lead the list of those struck by lightning because they are often out on the course when a storm comes, and they have nowhere to go. Hikers are second on the list.

Since lightning will take the path of least resistance, you want to avoid things that are good conductors of electricity, like water. Standing on or near water is a bad idea. So is standing near metal objects. Neither will attract a lightning bolt, but should one hit nearby, the electrical current from the strike is more likely to travel through the water or metal object. Also avoid standing in the mouth of a cave or alcove. Electricity might just jump the gap from the ceiling of the cave to the floor, using you like a spark plug.

Note: Interestingly enough, dry snow is actually a poor conductor of electricity due to all the air space contained within it.

So what should you do if you're caught out in a lightning storm? Well, hanging out in a thick grove of trees would be my first choice—hopefully underneath my tarp reading a good book in my sleeping bag. Unfortunately this is not always an option. Next best is to be in the shadow of a large peak or canyon wall. By this, I don't mean the shadow caused by the sun. Rather, I mean that a tall, broad land feature may receive the lightning strikes up high above and dissipate them long

BZZZZZZ!

(A BAD SIGN)

before the current reaches you. So being in the bottom of a deep canyon or close to the base of a peak is safer than being out on an open plain or on top of a mesa.

If you find yourself caught out on a ridge with no chance to descend, your choices are limited. The best answer may be finding the lowest dry spot (gullies or crevices in the rock do not count because they may conduct ground current) and sit it out on top of your pack, Ensolite pad, or other non-conductive substance, scrunched up as small as possible. On an open plain look for a dry ditch or lie as low as possible on a non-conductive material.

If you are caught out in the open with others, then spread out. This way if one person gets struck, the others can help out, instead of all getting slammed. A lightning victim without a heartbeat may respond well to CPR.

Figuring Out the Weather

If you spend a lot of time hiking in one region, get into the habit of watching the weather patterns. Which way does the wind blow before a storm? What direction are the clouds moving before it clears off? Watching local weather patterns enables you to start predicting the weather, at least for the next few hours or so.

If you have a barometer (or altimeter), then use it to monitor the trends you see. This gives you an idea of how far of a drop you need to get before wet weather prevails. You will also be able to figure out how much lead time it gives you before the weather changes. I have been places where the barometer would drop eight hours before the storm came in. I have also watched the barometer change only minutes before it started raining.

Things I like to watch for:

- Are the jets flying over producing a contrail? If not, then the air at that altitude is dry enough so the cooling and compression of it, as it passes through the turbines, is not condensing any moisture. If the contrails are short, then whatever moisture is condensed is being quickly reabsorbed. Long contrails that last hours after the flight has gone by tell me a lot of moisture is aloft. Could a warm front be coming my way?

- Thin, wispy clouds aloft also suggest a warm front. If they continue to thicken throughout the day, I will be pitching my tent in the evening.

- A halo around the moon or sun also is an indication that moisture is aloft.

- Strong winds mean the weather is changing. If it has been cloudy and wet, then a high pressure system may be on its way.

- Early morning fog that burns off as the sun comes up means dry weather for the rest of the day.

- Where I live, wet weather generally comes out of the southwest. So anytime I see a long line of clouds building up from this direction I can assume I will need my umbrella.

- I love to watch the sunset. Since the weather where I live comes from a westerly direction, the last rays of the sun are passing through the air masses that will be with me overnight. If I see a dull or yellow sunset, then I know I should pitch my tarp because there is moisture coming my way. This is due to the fact that water vapor is absorbing the light in the red spectrum. On the other hand, if the sunset is a brilliant red with lots of alpenglow—well, let's just say I have only been disappointed once in my quest to sleep under the stars.

Leave No Trace (LNT)

The Leave No Trace program establishes a widely accepted code of outdoor ethics to shape a sustainable future for wildlands. Originating in the 1970s with the United States Forest Service, LNT was developed to help recreationists minimize their impacts while enjoying the outdoors. In 1991, the Forest Service teamed with the National Outdoor Leadership School (NOLS) and the Bureau of Land Management as partners in the Leave No Trace program. NOLS, a recognized leader in developing and promoting minimum-impact practices, began developing and distributing LNT educational materials and training.

Today, the non-profit organization Leave No Trace, Inc., established in 1994, manages the national program. LNT unites four federal land management agencies—the U.S. Forest Service, National Park Service, Bureau of Land Management, and U.S. Fish and Wildlife Service, with manufacturers, outdoor retailers, user groups, educators, and individuals who share a commitment to maintaining and protecting our natural lands for future enjoyment.

Plan Ahead and Prepare
- Know the regulations and special concerns for the area you'll visit.
- Prepare for extreme weather, hazards, and emergencies.
- Schedule your trip to avoid times of high use.
- Visit in small groups. Split larger parties into groups of four to six.
- Repackage food to minimize waste.
- Use a map and compass to eliminate the use of marking paint, rock cairns, or flagging.

Travel and Camp on Durable Surfaces
- Durable surfaces include established trails and campsites, rock, gravel, dry grasses, or snow.
- Protect riparian areas by camping at least 200 feet from lakes and streams.
- Good campsites are found, not made. Altering a site is not necessary.

In popular areas:
- Concentrate use on existing trails and campsites.
- Walk single file in the middle of the trail, even when wet or muddy.
- Keep campsites small. Focus activities in areas where vegetation is absent.

In pristine areas:
- Disperse use to prevent the creation of campsites and trails.
- Avoid places where impacts are just beginning.

Dispose of Waste Properly
- Pack it in, pack it out. Inspect your campsite and rest areas for trash or spilled foods. Pack out all trash, leftover food, and litter.
- Deposit solid human waste in catholes dug 6 to 8 inches deep at least 200 feet from water, camp, and trails. Cover and disguise the cathole when finished.

- Pack out toilet paper and hygiene products.
- To wash yourself or your dishes, carry water 200 feet away from streams or lakes and use small amounts of biodegradable soap. Scatter strained dishwater.

Leave What You Find

- Preserve the past: examine, but do not touch cultural or historic structures and artifacts.
- Leave rocks, plants, and other natural objects as you find them.
- Avoid introducing or transporting non-native species.
- Do not build structures or furniture or dig trenches.

Minimize Campfire Impacts

- Campfires can cause lasting impacts to the backcountry. Use a lightweight stove for cooking and enjoy a candle lantern for light.
- Where fires are permitted, use established fire rings, fire pans, or mound fires.
- Keep fires small. Only use sticks from the ground that can be broken by hand.
- Burn all wood and coals to ash, put out campfires completely, then scatter cool ashes.

Respect Wildlife

- Observe wildlife from a distance. Do not follow or approach them.
- Never feed animals. Feeding wildlife damages their health, alters natural behaviors, and exposes them to predators and other dangers.
- Protect wildlife and your food by storing rations and trash securely.
- Control pets at all times or leave them at home.
- Avoid wildlife during sensitive times: mating, nesting, raising young, or winter.

Be Considerate of Other Visitors

- Respect other visitors and protect the quality of their experience.
- Be courteous. Yield to other users on the trail.
- Step to the downhill side of the trail when encountering pack stock.
- Take breaks and camp away from trails and other visitors.
- Let nature's sounds prevail. Avoid loud voices and noises.

For more specifics about LNT and camping and traveling in specific ecological zones contact the Leave No Trace Office at 1-800-332-4100 (www.LNT.org) for a booklet on the zone you are interested in.

Other Recommended Resources

Conners, Tim and Christine, *Lipsmackin' Backpackin'*, Falcon Publishing, Helena, MT, 2000, 225 pages.

Crouch, Gregory, *Route Finding: Navigating With Map and Compass*, Falcon Publishing, Helena, MT, 1999, 96 pages.

Getchell, Annie, *The Essential Outdoor Gear Manual*, Ragged Mountain Press, Camden, ME, 1995, 260 pages.

Hampton, Bruce, Cole, David, *Soft Paths*, Stackpole Books, Mechanicsburg, PA, 1995, 222 pages.

Harmon, Will, *Wild Country Companion*, Falcon Publishing, Helena, MT, 1994, 195 pages.

Harvey, Mark, *The National Outdoor Leadership School's Wilderness Guide*, A Fireside Book, Simon and Schuster, New York, NY, 1999, 268 pages.

Jardine, Ray, *Beyond Backpacking*, Adventure Lore Press, LaPine, OR, 2000, 504 pages.

Kals, William S., *Land Navigation Handbook: The Sierra Club Guide to Map and Compass*, Sierra Club Books, 1983.

Kjellstrom, Bjorn and Heisley, Newt, *Be Expert With Map & Compass: The Complete Orienteering Handbook*, IDG Books Worldwide, 1994, 220 pages.

O'Bannon, Allen, and Clelland, Mike, *Allen and Mike's Really Cool Backcountry Ski Book*, Falcon Publishing, Helena, MT, 1996, 114 pages.

Schimelpfenig, Tod, and Lindsey, Linda, *NOLS Wilderness First Aid*, Stackpole Books, Harrisburg, PA, 1992, 356 pages.

Lindholm, Claudia, editor, *NOLS Cookery*, Stackpole Books, Mechanicsburg, PA, 1997, 150 pages.

Wilkerson, James A., Medicine for Mountaineering, The Mountaineers, Seattle, WA, 1990, 438 pages.

Woodmenecy, Jim, *Reading Weather*, Falcon Publishing, Helena, MT, 1998, 148 pages.

Other recommended readings

McManus, Patrick, *A Fine and Pleasant Misery*, Henry Holt and Company, New York, NY, 1978, 209 pages.

Rawicz, Slavomir, *The Long Walk*, Lyons and Buford, Publishers, New York, NY, 1984, 240 pages.

Gear

The gear you bring on any trip really depends on the type of trip you are doing and what the weather and environment will be like. For a summer trip down in the Grand Canyon, for instance, I wouldn't bring more than one warm layer. A very lightweight sleeping bag or sheet would be fine for sleeping. I would carry lots of water in my pack though. A late fall trip into the mountains will demand warmer clothes and more food. Don't be tied to this list. Use it as a baseline to help you determine what you need and don't need.

Personal gear

- [ ] backpack
- [ ] straps
- [ ] lightweight nylon day pack
- [ ] 3 to 4 upper-body layers
- [ ] 2 lower-body layers
- [ ] sun hat
- [ ] warm hat (w/tassle)
- [ ] 1 pair gloves and/or mittens (shells?)
- [ ] 5 pairs socks
- [ ] wind layers (shirt, pants)
- [ ] rain layers
- [ ] boots
- [ ] gaiters
- [ ] camp shoes
- [ ] sleeping bag
- [ ] Ensolite pad or Therm-a-rest (with stuff sack cover)
- [ ] sleeping bag stuff sack
- [ ] cup
- [ ] bowl
- [ ] spoon
- [ ] water bottle
- [ ] food bag
- [ ] sunglasses
- [ ] sunscreen
- [ ] 2 lighters
- [ ] candles
- [ ] headlamp
- [ ] bandanna
- [ ] bug dope and head net (for buggy places)
- [ ] toothbrush
- [ ] other toiletries

Luxury items

- [ ] Crazy Creek chair
- [ ] book
- [ ] camera
- [ ] umbrella
- [ ] ground cloth
- [ ] hiking sticks
- [ ] galoshes

Group gear

- [ ] this book!
- [ ] stove
- [ ] fuel
- [ ] tent or fly
- [ ] pot
- [ ] fry pan
- [ ] utensils
- [ ] water filter or disinfectant
- [ ] first-aid kit
- [ ] general repair kit
- [ ] maps
- [ ] compass
- [ ] ropes to hang food (if in bear country)

Index

A

accessibility, packing your backpack for 14–15
animals. *See* wildlife

B

backpacks
  adjusting 54–56
  day packs 26–27
  divided *vs.* top-loading 26
  internal *vs.* external frame 24, 25
  large *vs.* small 25, 26
  packing
    ABCs of 14–18
    balancing weight 15
    compressing contents 15–16
    developing your own system for 18
    filling empty spaces 15, 20
    fuel bottles 20
    organizing for accessibility 14–15
    potato sack method 19
    putting things inside *vs.* outside 16–18
    sleeping bags 18–19
    sleeping pads 17–18
    streamlining 16–18
    tents 19
    using stuff sacks 20
  putting on 52–54
  reducing pack weight 20–22
  simple *vs.* complex 25–26
  taking off 54
  waterproofing 22–23
baking bread products 85–87
balaclavas 7
balance, packing your backpack for 15
bathing 92
bears
  avoiding surprises 123
  backing away from 123–24
  bear canisters 128
  bear hangs 126, 127, 128, 129
  black 120, 121
  charging 125
  checking out the area beforehand 122–23
  climbing trees to avoid 124
  creating a distraction for 124
  discouraging bears in camp 126, 128–29
  and dogs 123
  encountering bears while hiking 123–24
  grizzly 120, 121
  hiking in a group 123
  making noises to warn 123
  mothers with cubs 120–21
  polar 120
  problem/habituated 121–22
  responding to an attack by 125
  running from 124
  using pepper spray to repel 125, 127
  watching for bear sign 123
  and wind direction 124
bivy bags 30–31
black bears. *See* bears
blisters. *See under* foot care
boiling water, to kill pathogens 88
boot & pack chart 32
boots
  importance of 31
  lacing 45
  selecting 31–33
  using gaiters 11, 34, 35
  waterproofing 33, 35
  See also foot care
bread recipes 86, 87
breathing, monitoring your 49
butane stoves 37, 81

C

cagoules 11, 12
campcraft
  baking bread products 85–87
  bathing 92
  "bombproofing" your campsite 78
  breaking camp 79
  camping in good style 1
  cleaning cooking utensils 92
  cooking on a fire 81–84
  cooking safely 85
  dealing with menstrual needs 93

checking your equipment 108
deciding on companions 103-4
defining goals 102-3
doing research
    asking the right questions 106
    finding out about permits
      and regulations 105
    getting good information
      104-5
    identifying potential hazards
      106
    learning about possible
      weather 106
    planning transportation
      106-7
estimating fuel needs 114-15
food planning 109-14
getting companions committed
    103-4
identifying a leader 104
learning first aid 116-17
leaving your itinerary with a friend
    116
obtaining maps 115
planning for emergencies 116-17
resolving equipment issues 108
setting a budget 104
taking dogs 107-8
pooping. *See* human waste, disposing of
propane stoves 37

R
rabies 120
rain, hiking in 10-12, 57
rain flies 38-40
regulations, learning about 105
repair kits 41
river crossings
    dry crossings 134
    falling in the water 141
    finding the best spot for 132
    following your intuition 140
    hazards of 133
    high-stepping crossings 135
    timing of 139
    unbuckling your waist belt 139
    using a boat 140
    using a rope 134, 140
    using a spotter 139
    wet crossings
      factors to consider 136-37
      4 person method 138

handholding chain technique
    138
strategies for 137-38
3 person tripod 140
train technique 139
wearing boots 138
rock fields, crossing
    scree, talus, and hardpan slopes
      145
    tips for 142-44
    walking across boulders 144-45

S
sanitary pads, disposing of 93
searching for lost persons 131
shoes, camp 8
shorts 6
Simple Quick Bread recipe 86
Simple Yeast Bread recipe 87
single-walled tents, *vs.* double-walled
    39-40
sleeping bags
    design tips 28-29
    down-filled 27
    loft in 28
    packing 18-19
    with synthetic fill 28
    temperature ratings for 28
sleeping pads
    closed-cell *vs.* open-cell foam pads
      29-30
    inflatable 30
    packing 17-18
    purposes of 29
socks 7-8, 45
staking 73, 75
stoves 37, 79-81
streamlining, in packing your backpack
    16-18
stuff sacks, avoiding overuse of 20
sun protection
    checklist for 13
    clothing for desert hiking 13
    hankies as 7
synthetic fabrics 4

T
tampons, disposing of 93
tarps
    advantages *vs.* disadvantages of
      38-39

The Author

Allen O'Bannon started his backpacking career in Oregon and has since lugged a pack all around the western U.S., including Alaska. He has also taken a couple of excursions to Chile and Africa. Currently he is a program supervisor for the National Outdoor Leadership School (where much of his learning took place working as an outdoor educator) in Victor, Idaho. In addition to his search for everlasting peace, he would appreciate your vote for his 2004 presidential campaign.

The Illustrator

Mike Clelland! never went to art school, studying *Mad* magazine instead. Mike grew up in the flat plains of Michigan, then spent ten years (as a Yuppie!) in New York City. In 1987 he thought it might be fun to be a ski bum in Wyoming for the winter. Unfortunately, after living and skiing in the Rockies, he found it quite impossible to return to his previous life in the Big City. Mike is presently living an eco-groovy life in a shed in Idaho where he divides his time between illustrator and NOLS instructor.